Advance Praise for

FAKING IT

"This book is a brilliant and necessary part of the conversation, and it cements Alptraum as one of our most essential contemporary voices on sex and gender."
—Carmen Maria Machado, author of
Her Body and Other Parties

"Quite literally a revelation....Alptraum sets a cleansing fire to myths about sex, shame, and deception that have been hiding in plain sight for centuries."
—Andi Zeisler, author of *We Were Feminists Once*

"This is a mindblower of a read. A completely fresh perspective."
—Jenny Lumet, screenwriter, *Rachel Getting Married*

"Lux Alptraum is a fearless and frequently hilarious guide through the murky waters of twenty-first century sexual politics, one who never settles for the easy answers. *Faking It* shows that in sex—as in so much else—what women do matters less than why they do it."
—Sady Doyle, author of *Trainwreck*

"[*Faking It*] should be required reading."
—Emma Sulkowicz, artist

FAKING IT

FAKING IT

The Lies Women Tell About Sex—
and the Truths They Reveal

LUX ALPTRAUM

SEAL PRESS

Seal Press

Hachette Book Group

1290 Avenue of the Americas, New York, NY 10104

www.sealpress.com

@sealpress

Printed in the United States of America

First Edition

Published by Seal Press, an imprint of Perseus Books, LLC, a subsidiary of Hachette Book Group, Inc. The Seal Press name and logo is a trademark of the Hachette Book Group.

The publisher is not responsible for websites (or their content) that are not owned by the publisher.

Print book interior design by Six Red Marbles

Certain names and identifying characteristics have been changed

Library of Congress Cataloging-in-Publication Data

Names: Alptraum, Lux, author.
Title: Faking it : the lies women tell about sex—and the truths they reveal / Lux Alptraum.
Description: New York, NY : Seal Press, 2018. | Includes bibliographical references.
Identifiers: LCCN 2018014655| ISBN 9781580057653 (pbk.) | ISBN 9781580057660 (e-book)
Subjects: LCSH: Women—Sexual behavior. | Sex. | Deception.
Classification: LCC HQ29 .A47 2018 | DDC 306.7082—dc23
LC record available at https://lccn.loc.gov/2018014655

ISBNs: 978-1-58005-765-3 (paperback), 978-1-58005-766-0 (e-book)

LSC-C

10 9 8 7 6 5 4 3 2 1

*For women everywhere: the liars,
the truth tellers, and especially
the survivors.*

A Note on Language

THIS BOOK DEALS with historical and cultural ideas of womanhood and sex, many of which are born out of a conception of "women" as people with breasts, vaginas, and uteruses. However, nothing in this book is intended to imply that all people with vaginas are women, that all women have vaginas, or that there is one universal definition that encompasses all women. Sexuality, gender, and biological sex are infinitely complex topics, and any attempt at generalization will always be incomplete.

Contents

Introduction

Faking It

ON NOVEMBER 9, 2016, I awoke with a sense of despair. After a brutal, months-long presidential campaign, America had chosen its new leader. And rather than select a former secretary of state, senator, and first lady—perhaps the most qualified person ever to run for the position—we'd gone with a real estate magnate turned reality show star who'd risen to prominence on a wave of hatred, empty promises, and deceit.

To cap it all off, a significant number of voters had come through the election believing that it was Donald Trump who was the more honest and trustworthy candidate; that Hillary Rodham Clinton was, as Trump had cried numerous times throughout the year, just "Crooked Hillary," a woman more worthy of a prison cell than a political appointment. Never mind that the award-winning fact-checking website Politifact's scorecard calculates that Trump told the whole, unvarnished truth just 4 percent of the time (compared to Clinton's 24 percent), or that former *New York Times* executive editor Jill Abramson had declared Clinton to be "fundamentally honest and trustworthy." In the eyes of a significant portion of the electorate, Clinton was not to be trusted.

That morning, as the reality of the election results began to sink in, I felt devastated, but not exactly surprised. As much as it broke my heart to see Clinton rejected in favor of Trump, the criticisms that had paved the path toward her defeat—that she was untrustworthy, manipulative, and duplicitous—were ones I was intimately familiar with. And not merely because they were accusations that had been hurled at Clinton for the entirety of her time in the public eye, but because being accused of dishonesty is a fundamental part of growing up as a woman in America.

The idea that women are liars is deeply ingrained into American culture—particularly when it comes to sex. In the common telling, women are duplicitous seductresses, gifted with a particular talent for bending the truth to pull one over on men. We alter our appearances to make ourselves more attractive, we erase whole sections of our sexual pasts in order to seem more demure. We feign disinterest, we fake our orgasms, and when it's all said and done, we "cry rape" in an attempt to destroy whatever man has done us wrong.

When I first started thinking seriously about the topic of women and deceit, I was convinced that we women had merely been victims of a particularly vicious smear campaign, one that unfairly cast aspersions on our fundamental honesty. Surely, I thought, the idea of the duplicitous female was nothing more than an invention of men, one intended to discredit women and keep us in check and out of power. Surely, I thought, the notion that women are gaming the system was a vicious myth with little to no basis in truth.

But as I began to dig, it quickly became apparent how wrong my initial assessment was.

It's true that the world is full of women who, like Secretary Clinton, are presumed to be peddling fiction when we're actually offering up fact. But it's also true that—whether it's fake orgasms, artificial hymens, or suspiciously spotless sexual pasts—there are many instances in which women *are* lying. And while a number of honorable women have been unfairly slandered as dishonest, it's the lies that many, if not most, of us are telling on a daily basis that offer the greater insight into the female experience.

We lie because it makes our day-to-day lives easier; we lie to keep ourselves safe; we lie because no one believes us when we tell the truth. But most of all, we lie because the world expects us to live up to an impossible standard—and frequently, lying is the only way to get through life with our sanity intact.

The question isn't whether women are trustworthy. The question is why women lie—and what those lies are trying to tell us.

❚ CHAPTER ONE ❚

I Just Came

A SHORT WALK from my home on the Lower East Side of Manhattan lies Katz's Delicatessen, one of the neighborhood's biggest tourist attractions. It's possible you've heard of Katz's because of its famous pastrami sandwiches. But it's equally likely you know it for reasons completely unrelated to its food: Katz's is the site of the famous "I'll have what she's having" scene from *When Harry Met Sally*, a moment so iconic the restaurant even has a sign noting where, exactly, Meg Ryan's famed fake orgasm took place.

It's strange that a brief scene from an old film defines a place that's been featured in over a dozen movies and TV shows. But the staying power of the *When Harry Met Sally* scene is almost definitely due to its unabashed look at a topic that manages to be intriguing, taboo, and incredibly controversial: the faked female orgasm. Whether you think it's a harmless fib or a major faux pas, there's no denying that "faking it" is inextricably connected to our ideas about female sexuality. When newly out trans woman Caitlyn Jenner received a lesson in fake orgasm in the second season of reality show *I Am Cait*, the implication was clear. As TMZ succinctly put it, "Caitlyn Jenner is learning what it means to be a woman."

The specter of feigned female pleasure is ever present, with women's magazines and sex educators chiding women who turn to ersatz orgasm when the real thing remains elusive, and men's magazines so preoccupied with tips for determining whether a partner is truly enjoying herself that it often seems like men are convinced that any woman who seems to orgasm might, in fact, be faking. Occasionally there's even a personal essay from a woman who's finally fessing up to her fakery, usually with a healthy dose of contrition.

But while all this obsession with orgasmic authenticity is at least partially justified—faked orgasms can, and do, happen during sex—much of the conversation around faking it seems to be missing the point. Sussing out the real orgasms from the fake ones, or getting women to take a solemn oath never to fake again, might feel like minor victories, but they don't even begin to scratch the surface of the truly important question here. Namely: Why do women even fake orgasms in the first place?

The typical read on fake orgasms is a simple one: women fake because they're having subpar sex and want to get it over with. In this version of events, women don't understand their bodies, or are bad at communicating their needs, or end up partnering with men who don't listen, and the result is unsatisfying sex (at least for the woman). Hoping to keep the peace with her partner—or perhaps just get some bad sex over and done with—the woman spares everyone embarrassment by mimicking the signs of sexual pleasure. Women are crafty manipulators, but it's ultimately to their disadvantage: sure, they've tricked a man into thinking he's done well, but at the cost of their own sexual fulfillment.

It's this interpretation of faked pleasure that's led to so many campaigns against faking it. If only women could be more in touch with their physical pleasure, could speak about their needs more, could advocate for their own orgasms, no one would need to fake. Taken to the extreme, this argument means women who fake aren't merely letting themselves down: they're actively traitors to the feminist movement, upholding mythical ideas about what women want from sex, and convincing legions of men that their selfish sexual technique is that of a giving, generous lover.

But is it really quite so cut-and-dry? Is the female urge to fake purely about preserving male ego at the expense of a woman's access to enjoyment—or are there other, more complicated reasons why a woman might feign an orgasm when she isn't actually feeling it? Is the act of faking an orgasm truly a betrayal of the fight for women's sexual liberation, or is it, perhaps, a way of claiming control over a sexual situation? Why is the authenticity of anyone's orgasm worth discussing to begin with?

What is an orgasm? What does it feel like? How do you know if you've had one?

If you have a penis, the answers to these questions are presumably straightforward. An orgasm is the sensation that accompanies ejaculation, and it feels, you know, pretty great. Because male orgasm is associated with ejaculation,[1] few men devote much time to worrying about whether or not they've *actually* had one. The proof is—if you'll pardon the turn of phrase—in the pudding.

If you have vulva, on the other hand, the situation is a bit different. During the mid-twentieth century, pioneering sexologists William Masters and Virginia Johnson attempted to map out the "typical" female sexual response cycle, dividing

---

[1] Though, contrary to popular belief, not the same process.

it into four distinct stages: excitement, plateau, orgasm, and resolution. Under the model, the female sexual response cycle can be broadly understood as analogous to its male counterpart: penises get erect; vulvae lubricate. Muscles in the genital regions swell and contract, then release in a series of orgasmic pulses; post-orgasm, the body begins to cool down and relax.

There is value in the Masters and Johnson model, and it certainly describes the physical experience of some women (certainly enough so that doctors are still making use of it to diagnose sexual disorders). Yet in the decades since its debut, this linear, four-stage model has come under a great deal of criticism. It makes broad assumptions about the similarities between male and female sexual response. It primarily focused on women who were able to orgasm during penis-in-vagina intercourse, reinforcing the idea that that one particular sex act is central to female sexual pleasure while simultaneously devaluing the nonorgasmic pleasures derived from penis-in-vagina sex. In the decades since, a number of other sex researchers have attempted to map out female sexual response with other models: circular rather than linear models and models that include desire, emotional intimacy, and other nonphysical aspects of sexual pleasure. But even as these models improve on the work of Masters and Johnson, it's still difficult to create one model of sexual ecstasy that can assuredly guide a woman on the path to orgasm (and guarantee that she'll know when she's had one) because of one very simple fact: there's no one universal sign that serves as an indicator of female sexual ecstasy.

This fact can create a challenge for aspiring female orgasmers, particularly since orgasm isn't an experience that we're easily able to describe. "How would you describe what tickling feels like?" asks Charlie Glickman, a Seattle-based sex and relationships coach with two decades of experience in sex education, including a stint as the education program manager at San Francisco–based sex shop Good Vibrations. "How can you describe what chocolate tastes like? We don't actually have a definition for these things. All we can do is give someone a piece of chocolate, or tickle them, and say, that's the sensation that I'm talking about."

But orgasms aren't as readily available, or easily distributed, as bars of chocolate—and if you're a preorgasmic woman, desperate to figure out how you'll *know* when it happens, it's understandable that you might turn to porn or romance novels or *Cosmopolitan* or even *Our Bodies, Ourselves* in search of some information that might help you better understand what, exactly, the elusive O is, and how you'll know when (or if) you've achieved it.

I was introduced to the concept of orgasm not by a lady mag or swoony romance novel but by Peter Mayle's *Where Did I Come From?*, a seventies-era entrant into the genre of sex ed books for kids. If you haven't had the privilege of leafing through this classic, it is *very* seventies, with a straightforward approach to the facts about doing it and a whole lot of illustrations of a chubby, vaguely Semitic-looking couple whose naked bodies are presumably intended to stand in for those of your parents.

Where Did I Come From? does not shy away from topics like pleasure. Sex, Mayle wants children to know, is a very lovely experience—akin to "a gentle tingly sort of tickle"— one that culminates in "a tremendous big lovely shiver" for everyone involved (Mayle is rather bullish on the possibility of simultaneous orgasm). For readers still curious to know what, exactly, this "shiver" feels like, Mayle follows up with an aside that notes that "it's not easy to tell you what this feels like. But you know how it is when you have a tickle in your nose for a long time, and then you have a really big sneeze? It's a little like that." On the opposite page, there's an illustration of a sneezing baby accompanied by a caption that reads, "It feels a bit like this, but much better."

It's easy to mock this notion of orgasm as a sneeze, only better (I myself have mocked it on many, many occasions). But Mayle's attempt to describe the sensation of coming is about as good as most others, especially when you factor in that he's somewhat stymied by the fact that he's trying to offer R-rated insights to kids.

And the idea of orgasm as a sneeze-plus is at least less vague—and much more realistic—than a number of the other conceptions out there. Here are some of the descriptions of orgasm I've heard in my discussions with women: Mia, who learned about orgasm through watching porn, told me she'd been primed to expect a "big ordeal that came with bells and whistles" that served as a "big finish" to the act of sex (though what, exactly, was causing that big ordeal, or what exactly it felt like, remained pretty mysterious to her). Ruby told me that as an adolescent, she knew orgasm "was supposed to feel like a 'build up and release' and that there would be full-body pleasure," while Rebecca, a twenty-seven-year-old sex blogger, had heard it was "an explosion that ran through your body," but was convinced it could only happen during penis-in-vagina intercourse. Amanda Rose, a twenty-three-year-old PhD student who'd been sexually active for a few years before learning about orgasms in her late teens, wrote in her high school journal that she'd heard orgasm was "a tingly feeling all over your body" and "like you really have to pee."[2]

Not surprisingly, the most vivid descriptions of orgasm tend to be found in romance novels. A thirty-year-old social worker told me that her adolescent exploration of the genre gave her "a vague, if somewhat glorified idea of what an orgasm was. It seemed like such a mind-shattering, earth-breaking thing when a woman had an orgasm, and I was reading [about] it, so it must be true, right?"

If you've never delved into the genre yourself, here's a sampling of what sort of orgasmic descriptions are on offer. Some writers opt for airborne metaphors: orgasm makes you "grow wings, defy gravity and your soul slips quietly across the universe like a shooting star" (Chloe Thurlow). Others are drawn to more fiery descriptions, offering that it feels like "searing heat, electric pulses surging through my body and my soul, as our orgasms burst forth together, a million nerve endings suddenly flashing like twin rockets exploding fireworks, the multitude of sparks joining with a billion stars in the heavens above" (Simone Freier). Still others go the floral route: "something blossomed deep within and opened almost like the multiple petals of a rose, pushing back the tension in rippling waves as they bloomed until she surrendered to relaxation with a soft exclamation of surprise" (Mary Balogh).

A *Cosmopolitan* piece surveying women about their experience of the big O isn't much better: opening with a somewhat snide comment about women who "think" they've had

---

[2] The notion of a relationship between female orgasm and urination is a fairly common one, particularly when you factor in the possibility of female ejaculation. Not surprisingly, hearing that orgasm might feel like wetting the bed leaves more than a few women feeling a bit nervous about the experience.

orgasms ("if you have to use the word *think*, it ain't happening"), the piece goes on to offer descriptions as vague and
variant as "an overwhelming feeling of tingles throughout
your body," "like a volcanic eruption...but down there," "every ounce of sexual energy being sucked from my body,"
"like filling a glass of water until it overflows," and "a blend
of dancing and riding the craziest rollercoaster ever."

You could be forgiven if all this orgasm talk makes your
head swim (the same way your head presumably swims
during orgasm), and you could especially be forgiven if it
leaves you feeling more confused than ever about the dynamics of sexual climax. If you're young and preorgasmic,
learning that orgasm is like a sneeze but also fireworks and
flying and definitely something you'll recognize when you
experience it (assuming you don't get confused and accidentally wet the bed), and, most importantly of all, the
greatest and best experience ever, isn't particularly helpful—
especially if most of that doesn't quite turn out to be true.

Yes, in spite of all the hype, there are plenty of orgasms
that aren't all that exciting, let alone awe inspiring or life
changing. The notion of an underwhelming orgasm goes
against everything we think we know about sex, but climaxes that aren't particularly explosive are much more
common than we think. Granted, it's rare to find women
speaking publicly about the phenomenon—but that's likely
because, well, admitting your orgasms aren't amazing feels a
bit like branding yourself a failure.

Despite *Cosmopolitan*'s conviction that any woman who's
had an orgasm absolutely knows for sure, the extreme
hype around erotic release leaves a number of women baffled that what feels like a sexual finish isn't living up to the
hype. As Ruby told me, "When I had my first clitoral orgasm,

I didn't even realize I'd had one." Contrary to what she'd been led to expect, her first few dozen orgasms were rather unimpressive—so weak, in fact, that after they occurred she attempted to soldier on in pursuit of that magical explosion, deterred only by the fact that her post-orgasmic clitoris was far too sensitive to continue stimulating. "There was a build-up, but the peak was so faint and so pin-point—nothing like the crazy full-body experience I'd heard about," she told me.

Ruby isn't the only woman to experience a less-than-mind-blowing orgasm. Another woman's description of her early orgasms—posted in the LiveJournal community Vagina Pagina—notes that "at a certain point, when everything feels *really* good, it feels like my vagina (and inner parts) hiccup repeatedly, rhythmically, and involuntarily. Afterwards, my bits continue to randomly twitch for about ten minutes or so, or at least it feels like they twitch." (I'm a bit partial to this description of orgasm as it's reminiscent of my inaugural orgasmic experience—one that left me more befuddled than awash in the sort of warm glow that erotica had primed me to expect.)

Many women who feel led astray by the orgasm glorification complex are confused when sexual sensations don't live up to the storybook explosions and over-the-top thrashing and moans. Sarah, a thirty-seven-year-old 911 dispatcher whose first orgasm arrived during an erotic dream—"I woke up to my body spasming, and I had all the other physical indicators of having orgasmed," she told me—felt deeply confused after discovering the reality of orgasm. "My anticipation of orgasm was more of the moaning, screaming type that is depicted in [soft-core pornography]. I did not expect any of the feelings I had, the physical and the emotional, and I didn't expect it to be so 'quiet,' for lack of another term."

And the disconnect can be even greater for women who experience orgasm before they've been educated about what, exactly, it is and how it relates to sex. Hannah, a twenty-eight-year-old artist, discovered the joys of self-pleasure in early childhood, bringing herself to orgasm through the rhythmic contraction of her pelvic muscles. It wasn't until her late teens that she realized that this activity (which she'd long thought of as "stretching") was actually a sort of proto-masturbation. Realizing that the much hyped experience of sexual climax was little more than her childhood relaxation strategy was, she told me, "a bit of a letdown."

"There was a bit of 'Oh, that's it? That's an orgasm? That's what everyone's so obsessed with?'" she explained. "I thought that what people were feeling when they orgasmed must be a huge, massive, life-changing thing to justify how much it influenced people's actions and caused them to chase it so much. Realizing orgasms were really the same as this little thing I would do when I was bored left me so confused at society's obsession with it."

Lady mags and sex advice columnists often treat women who come forward about their underwhelming O's as objects of pity or people in need of a fix—better technique, perhaps, or breathing exercises or a deeper emotional connection with a partner or a different kind of vibrator. Yet while solid B orgasms might not be the kind of thing you hear about in *Cosmo* (I checked: none of the respondents refer to the feeling of orgasm as "kind of weird, like my vagina wants to grab things but keeps losing its grip," the way a teenage me might have), they're no less legitimate an orgasm than all the exploding showers of rose petals we keep hearing about.

Because an orgasm, as it happens, isn't one specific thing. To the extent that orgasm can be assigned any singular, universal categorization, it's that—as Emily Nagoski writes in *Come As You Are*—"orgasm is the sudden, involuntary release of sexual tension," a description that, yes, feels about as underwhelming as those introductory orgasms women told me about.

There are as many different types of orgasm as there are female bodies. Some orgasms are brought about by vaginal stimulation, others by the much ballyhooed clitoral stimulation, still others by nipple play or anal sex or even just standing around in the rain. Some women have the ability to orgasm by thinking themselves off—bringing themselves to sexual ecstasy just through sheer concentration. And while many of these climaxes are accompanied by the telltale vaginal contractions often associated with orgasm, that's not a guarantee (if it was, this chapter would be much, much shorter).

The one thing uniting all these orgasms? A certain sense of completion, which may or may not be accompanied by an explosive, overwhelming, full-body sensation. Yet it's rare to hear orgasm discussed as, "You know, that feeling when you're having sex and everything feels super exciting and tingly and then suddenly your body relaxes and is all, 'Nope, I'm done now,'" perhaps because that doesn't really make for the most exciting copy for a romance novel.

But perhaps we should start rethinking that. Because our intense romanticization of the grand climax isn't just inaccurate but actively works to prevent people (and, in particular, women) from enjoying sex. Not all orgasms are elaborate, intense affairs, but when we discuss them in that way, we create one more potentially unattainable goal for women to live up to. It's not enough to just focus on what feels good and leaves you happy and relaxed and connected to your partner. If your pleasure isn't dialed up to eleven each and every time, are you really living your best life?

Well, if you're feeling fulfilled and happy with the sex you're having, then absolutely, yes. Even if—blasphemous as it may sound—that fulfilling sexual experience doesn't actually end in orgasm.

"We've gone from 'People have sex for procreation' to 'People have sex to have orgasm,'" says Erin Basler, MEd, a staff member at Rhode Island's Center for Sexual Pleasure and Health. Basler notes that she doesn't really think that either of those sexual motivations has ever been universally true. The long history of birth control makes it abundantly clear that making babies has never really been the primary reason modern humans have pursued sex with one another. But if orgasm isn't the primary motivation for getting busy, then what, exactly, is?

Basler offers up a number of different reasons why someone might enjoy, or pursue, sex that they're pretty sure won't lead to orgasm. There's the thrill of physical intimacy, the desire to make another person happy, the stress-relieving potential—and, of course, the fact that the nonorgasm parts of sex can feel pretty good too. Fundamentally, we have sex "because touching erogenous zones feels good," she tells me—and while we've been conditioned to see the experience as a task-oriented one, it's also possible to treat it as an "experimental process" or "a journey that may just loop back around on itself," Möbius strip style.

Conversations I've had with women about their sex lives back up Basler's assertions. Julia, a thirty-two-year-old based in London who's more easily able to achieve orgasm through masturbation than sex, noted that "a sexual experience for me is about everything *but* the orgasm." What does that include? The ego boost of watching a partner get turned on by her body, the feeling of skin-to-skin contact, the pleasure of having someone celebrate and admire her vulva. Ruby made a distinction between her "sex drive" and her "orgasm drive," explaining that, "when I have sex, I certainly require pleasure, but I don't require orgasm. So as long as my partner's penis is hitting me at a good angle for a good amount of time, I'm happy." That appreciation for penetration was echoed by Amanda Rose, whose ability to orgasm is directly correlated to where she is in her menstrual cycle. As she told me, "getting rhythmically banged out"[3] can still feel great even when she knows orgasm isn't likely, or even possible; on nights when she wants to sleep well, but isn't feeling particularly horny, orgasm-free sex can be a useful way to relieve tension, relax, and get herself to sleep. Barbara, a twenty-two-year-old designer from Venezuela, described the thrill of "you and your partner in a naked tangle of limbs nuzzling and kissing and licking, exploring each other's bodies and whispering inside jokes and love words, smelling their hair and smacking their butt—orgasms I can have all by myself, but not that."

Other women talked up sex as an opportunity to provide a partner with pleasure. Sarah, who notes that "I'm not really a physical touch person but my husband is," compared sex to the household tasks her husband performs for her to make

---

[3] A phrase that, she noted, is a reference to the 2014 film *Obvious Child*.

her feel loved.[4] For Julia, who spoke in detail about her love of semen, a male partner's orgasm plays a bigger part in her enjoyment of a sexual experience than her own erotic release. That thrill of getting someone else off was echoed by the thirty-year-old social worker I spoke with, who told me, "My goal is to turn my partner on as much as possible and get them to orgasm. If I can edge for a bit and get the sensations to build enough so they have a stronger orgasm, then that's even better. . . . One of my kinks is that I really like to watch my partner get off."[5]

Indeed, reducing sex to nothing more than a fervent quest for orgasm has the effect of flattening a complex, nuanced experience of intimacy, connection, and pleasure. Most of us have an easier time achieving climax on our own than with a partner, and yet we're still driven to have sex with other people—a fact that suggests that, in our heart of hearts, we're aware that easy access to orgasm alone is not the be-all and end-all of why we get busy. So it shouldn't be that huge a leap to appreciate that not everyone has to have a mind-blowing (or even mediocre) orgasm in order to be fulfilled each and every time they have sex. And yet we still continue to emphasize orgasm as the primary, if not entire, purpose for pursuing sex—a sentiment that suggests that anyone who isn't able, or doesn't want, to achieve orgasm is some kind of freak or failure.

---

[4] Orgasm, on the other hand, is like "eating a cake"—though for Sarah, actively pursuing orgasm makes it difficult to achieve.

[5] It is interesting to note that, in many feminist circles, a man who professes a desire to pleasure his female partner with no concern for his own orgasm is considered a hero while a heterosexual woman in the same circumstances is portrayed as a victim. Given the historical tendency to deprioritize female pleasure, there's a certain logic to this—but it also puts feminist partner pleasers in a rather awkward position.

But anorgasmic women can, and do, have fulfilling sex lives. Tessa, a thirty-two-year-old nursing student who's been having sex since the age of fourteen, told me she's never had an orgasm and isn't particularly bothered by it.

Not that she's *never* been bothered by it, mind you. Over her eighteen years of sexual activity, Tessa's tried a number of "fixes": oral sex, dildos, vibrators—even the legendary Hitachi Magic Wand failed to produce anything magical (though Tessa notes that it is "fun to play with"). Baffled friends have offered unsolicited advice (including the deeply misguided tip that weight loss would make her orgasmic); partners have huffily declared sex with her to be "boring" and pointless[6] given the impossibility of orgasm.

Tessa can't pinpoint an exact moment when her frustration with anorgasmia gave way to self-acceptance ("it was more of a natural progression," she noted over email), but these days she's happy to pursue sex for all of its nonorgasmic joys ("A good sexual experience is one where afterwards I feel more connected to my sex partner"). In fact, her biggest problem with anorgasmia isn't the lack of orgasms: it's partners who see a sexual experience with her as a "challenge" or a puzzle to be solved, rather than an opportunity to intimately and honestly connect.

Experiences like Tessa's are more common than you might think: studies have suggested that upwards of 15 percent of women find themselves unable to orgasm. And it's

---

[6] Tessa's not the only woman to report being shamed by a partner for her anorgasmia. While the sentiment presumably comes from a good place—namely, the idea that sex should be pleasurable for both parties—it nevertheless reduces a woman's role in sex to orgasm-producing machine. There's a certain irony that both feminists and misogynists seem to see a woman's main goal in sex to be the creation of orgasm, diverging only over whose orgasm she should be investing her energies in.

not necessarily because they aren't doing it right, or haven't tried hard enough, or just need to find the right partner. Sometimes orgasms are absent because of health concerns—diabetes and multiple sclerosis can both affect the female sexual response cycle—or because of the medications a woman happens to be taking (in a perverse twist, hormonal contraception can put a damper on one's orgasmic capabilities). Depression can make orgasm elusive, as can antidepressants. Any number of things can interfere with orgasmic ability, and they're not all fixed by a long, relaxing bath and a good session with a vibrator.

Granted, as any worthwhile sexpert will tell you, a lack of orgasm is only a problem if you, personally, think it is. Orgasms aren't medically necessary, they're a fun bonus to a sexual experience, and if you're fine without them, well, then go forth and enjoy your orgasm-free sex life. In theory, anorgasmic women who are able to have enjoyable sex even sans orgasm should be able to acknowledge their situation and pursue sex on their own terms. Yet in our orgasm-obsessed culture, that's not always easy—as evidenced by the frustrations of women who are able to orgasm but sometimes choose not to.

Erika Moen, the creator of the sex toy review comic *Oh Joy Sex Toy*, is a tremendous fan of orgasm, saying that her first orgasmic experience—which came courtesy of a $10 vibrator purchased at a local sex toy shop—"changed my world.... It was so instantaneous and so encompassing, and I'd never experienced anything like it before. It was the very first time that I loved my body."

Perhaps counterintuitively, that life-changing intensity is the very reason why achieving orgasm isn't always her

priority when she's having sex—or even masturbating.[7]
"That first orgasm was totally mind blowing and wonderful
and life changing. But I don't want to have a life-changing
experience every time I have sex," she says. Sometimes it's
nice to just be able to feel intimate with her husband—or
with herself—without the draining, and overwhelming, experience of orgasm. Especially since the celebrated, mind-
blowing orgasm has some rarely discussed downsides: when
Moen is incredibly turned on, "I will come so hard and so
long…that it gets painful"—so painful, in fact, that she has
to take a break to recover.

Moen would love to speak more publicly about her
orgasm-optional attitude toward sex—perhaps even penning
a comic that reminds people that orgasms aren't required
for sex to be enjoyable—but she's all too aware that, in the
current climate, deprioritizing female orgasm gets immediately equated with deprioritizing female pleasure. And it's
not hard to understand why that is. After centuries of sexual
pleasure being treated as the exclusive domain of men, with
female orgasm barely acknowledged or treated as optional,
it feels important to tip the balance and bring forth a bit of
sexual equality.[8] But as female orgasm shifts from being a
myth to a bonus to a priority to a mandatory requirement,
it's women themselves who end up in a bind. As Ruby puts

---

[7] If the idea of enjoyable, orgasm-free sex is counterintuitive in American culture, the idea of enjoyable, orgasm-free masturbation is even more so. But in the
same way that sex can be a way of destressing and connecting with a partner,
even without some climactic fireworks, masturbation can be a way of relaxing
and reconnecting with one's self—even if there's no big payoff at the end.

[8] Which, it should be noted, is often framed in terms remarkably similar to those
of feminist fights. Pay equity advocates talk about the "wage gap" between men
and women; pleasure equity advocates bemoan the "orgasm gap."

it, "If you feel you *have* to have [an orgasm], it's not good any more. It's all great being in a fancy castle until you realize the gates are shut and you're trapped inside. Then you're just a prisoner."

Many women who enjoy sex without orgasm, or don't feel the need to come every time they get intimate with a partner, are fortunate enough to connect with understanding partners with an expansive understanding of what counts as "good sex." But for those whose partners have bought into the message that authentic sexual pleasure must always end in mutual orgasm—or, worse still, see a partner's orgasm as required proof of their own sexual prowess—sex can become a tiresome, unfun encounter. Alana Massey describes this especially exhausting class of sexual partner in a 2013 essay for *xoJane*:

> He is the gentleman caller that claims, "I'm sure I could make you come." . . . These are guys that barely know me, much less the inner workings of my lady business. While these men may feel like they're doing me a tremendous favor in their willingness to make an effort, what they are really saying is, "You may have lived in that body of yours for 27 years, but I am sure that I know my way around it better than you do!" And while I'll be as happy as a clam if they do eventually make me come, I want sex to be about the mutual enjoyment of each other's bodies without the man being preoccupied with some macho conquest that is more about his ego than my pleasure.

Tessa echoed this frustration, noting that, when she opens up to partners about her anorgasmia, "most of them take it as a challenge, which is frankly annoying." Given this reality, it's not that hard to see how, when faced with a partner who can't let go of the idea that a quality sexual experience must result in orgasms for all, a woman—especially one already enjoying a sexual experience—might not correct a partner who assumes her moans of pleasure are moans of orgasmic release, or might even outright fake it as a way to bring an end to a sexual experience without a lot of conversation about whether it was good enough and if she's actually feeling fulfilled.

Not all fakers have such complex motivations, however. There are plenty of women who fake orgasm as a way to put an end to subpar sex. As my friend, porn performer Ela Darling, put it to me, "Faking it preserves fragile male ego while also preserving the sanctity of my fragile vagina when we're playing, 'Let's all pretend you're as masterful at pussy as your profile says you are.'" Basler offers a more optimistic take on this premise, telling me that "people fake orgasms because they want the other person to feel good."

But while faking it is often about sparing, or boosting, a partner's feelings—no one's inclined to engage in theatrics when there isn't an audience present—it's not always about male sexual ineptitude. When we break away from our assumptions and ideals about sex—that "good" sex inherently implies orgasm for all involved, that sexual release is the only reason anyone engages in a sex act, that every act of intercourse occurs between two consenting adults with excellent communication skills and enough knowledge about their bodies to clearly express their physical needs—a number of more nuanced scenarios begin to emerge.

Most women fake it because orgasm is an "expected" part of the sexual script. But some women fake as a way of demonstrating that they *are* having a good time, even if genuine orgasm isn't imminent. Others fake because drugs or alcohol have made orgasm more elusive, and they're exhausted and ready to go to sleep. Still others fake because they've been pressured into sex and hope a feigned climax will bring an end to the experience. But if there's one truly common thread among all faked orgasms, it may be that—as the researchers behind a study presented at the 2016 British Psychological Society's Psychology of Women annual conference noted—faking orgasm "affords some control over ending a sexual encounter."

What does that control look like? Elisha, a young woman who contacted me over Twitter, offers one example. When Elisha started having sex with men, she was still preorgasmic— not an entirely uncommon occurrence in a society where young women aren't exactly encouraged to embark on solo explorations of their erogenous zones. But her lack of familiarity with orgasm didn't seem like a problem: after all, orgasms were supposed to be something that just naturally blossomed out of a woman in the course of a sexual experience, a magical explosion bursting forth just from the touch of the right man.

Except those magical, effortless orgasms didn't happen, and Elisha didn't quite know what to do. Guiding her partners through the intricacies of bringing her to orgasm wasn't an option—"I didn't know how to do it myself, much less help someone else to figure it out"—and merely telling a partner that what he was doing wasn't really working seemed likely to end up in hurt feelings and anger (neither of which felt likely to improve her sex life). Saying, "Hey, this was fun even though I didn't orgasm, but now I'm done and ready to stop," might have been the most *honest* solution, but since her orgasm felt mandatory, that approach never even occurred to her.

So she faked it.

Other women I spoke with—even ones who were experienced orgasmers—echoed the notion of ersatz orgasm as a strategic way of dictating the terms of a sexual encounter. Lisa is well aware of how to get herself to orgasm; as she explained to me, she's learned over time that she's "way more in control of my orgasm than anyone else" (apparently, it's largely a matter of how she positions her body). But she's not always up for a lengthy conversation about the various factors that need to be in play for the big O to arrive. And so when someone's "doing something that is well-intentioned but doesn't feel great and won't lead anywhere," she turns to fake orgasm as a convenient way to conclude that portion of the evening, without having to disrupt the mood with an awkward interjection and potentially uncomfortable conversation about the various flaws in her partner's technique.

It's easy to assume that this is all just the result of selfish, ignorant men who don't know how the female body works and aren't interested in taking the time to learn. Yet it's worth noting that women who have sex with women can—and do—fake it from time to time. Sage—who's faked with both men and women—told me that she's even faked it "with women I am really into or really enjoying having sex with." Why? "Most of the time I faked it was when I was with someone who didn't know me well enough, didn't know how I functioned or operated, what I do and don't like. When you meet someone for the first time, they might be very good at sex but they don't know those things that can really push you over the edge. Most of the time I would fake an orgasm to spare their feelings or because I know at the rate they are going it isn't going to happen."

This discomfort with the idea of stopping a sexual encounter—particularly a casual one, or one with a new partner—to launch a lengthy lecture about the specific techniques and tricks that will result in the greatest possible pleasure for everyone isn't something unique to these women, or even created by them. It's embedded in the way we describe good sex. As Basler reminds me, "We're all supposed to be naturally good at sex. The way the media portrays things, people just meet in bars and go fuck in a bathroom and everyone has great orgasms. But that's not how new partnerships work. You have to learn someone else's body, and you have to learn how the other person likes to be touched. You have to be able to teach people how to touch you. [I don't understand how] anyone has orgasms during one-night stands.... There's such a learning curve; it's basically like magic."

Yet it's a magic we see in most movie sex scenes (perhaps, not coincidentally, because most movies are directed by men). Think of how many times a movie or TV show has depicted sex as two bodies wordlessly colliding into one another in ecstasy, sparks flying with the mere hint of a caress. Now think of how many scenes involve awkward, detailed conversations during which one partner explains the specific sequence of stimulation patterns that'll result in an electrically charged experience—and where the other partner patiently, enthusiastically, takes in all the information, without getting frustrated or bored or annoyed at the delay. We're socially conditioned to see explicit sexual instruction as boring or mood killing—and when you're just looking to blow off steam or have some no-strings-attached, casual fun, it can be easier to eschew the big talk, enjoy the experience, and bring it to a close with a dramatic, fake finale.

Granted, advocating for fake orgasm as a way of avoiding conversation isn't something that's about to land in any sex educator's list of erotic best practices. We're *supposed* to be able to open up to, and honestly chat with, anyone we decide to go to bed with. In *theory*, sex is an act that we only engage in with people we trust enough to talk through the process of our arousal and climax. But those best practices require women to stage a solo offense against the idea that "good sex" is effortless and easy—a war that's more easily waged in the context of a trusting, committed relationship.

To actually hold ourselves to the standards of clearly communicating our needs to each and every partner, of taking the time to make sure we're getting exactly the stimulation our bodies require to reach the highest plains of pleasure, pretty much means no drunken hookups, no one-night stands, no casual encounters with a beautiful stranger we later realize we have nothing in common with. In short, it can mean radically reducing the ways in which women get to explore and express their sexuality, something quite a few women might find far more troubling than not orgasming during each and every sexual encounter.

In a somewhat paradoxical fashion, faked orgasm—the very thing that's supposed to symbolize sexually repressed and unfulfilled women—can offer women freedom from the rigid expectations their sex lives are often burdened with. To be sure, feigned pleasure isn't an ideal way of navigating a system that's supposed to be about intimacy and connection. But when we're conditioned to believe that that system must always be one where everything is effortless and unfolds in a seamless, romantic way; where bodies are supposed to conform to specific behaviors and patterns; and where orgasms are always desirable and always occur one specific way, fake orgasm can, ultimately, be a way out.

Why do women fake orgasms? Perhaps because we prioritize our ideas about what pleasure looks like over actual pleasure itself. Women get taught that orgasm is a mandatory requirement for good sex and that it's also supposed to be mind-blowingly fantastic, and should probably arrive while you're engaging in whatever sex act happens to be trendy at the time. If you're not readily orgasmic, or if your definition of good sex doesn't necessarily involve your own orgasmic release, or your orgasms aren't as earth shattering as they're "supposed" to be, the problem is with you and not with the cultural narrative itself.

And while it's tempting to write off faking as an easy out at best—or a betrayal of feminists at worst—perhaps we should be a little more generous toward the fakers among us. There's so much pressure on women to live our best sex lives: to be enthusiastic, adventurous, always up for it, and, of course, easily orgasmic. Yet there's so little space carved out for women to actually understand what that best sex life looks like for them, personally, as individuals, to buck against the narrative of acceptable sex and pleasure. Sometimes a fake orgasm is just a way of closing the gap between expectation and reality.

I would be remiss if I didn't mention that faking orgasm is not the sole domain of women. Men can—and do—fake orgasms, albeit not in quite the same numbers as women. A 2010 study appearing in the *Journal of Sex Research* found that a full 25 percent of male participants had faked (or, in the lingo of the study, "pretended") orgasm at some point in their sex lives; though that number is low in comparison to the 50 percent of women who reported faking it, it's far greater than the 0 percent that most people would assume.

If you're scratching your head wondering how, exactly, a man could fake an orgasm, as far as I know, no one's equipped their bedroom or overnight bag with an elaborate setup to simulate ejaculation in case of emergency. When men fake, they tend to rely on the same strategies as women, using moaning and exaggerated body motions to feign a climax. If a condom is in play, the absence of ejaculate tends to go unnoticed; if there's no condom in use, men can pretend to ejaculate inside their partner, or act as though they've orgasmed into their hand, or on a sheet, or somewhere that the lack of evidence won't be readily apparent.

Why do men fake? Largely for the same reasons as women. The above-mentioned study found that pretend orgasms occurred when a genuine orgasm was deemed unlikely, but the faker was ready to be done with sex and wanted to avoid hurting his partner's feelings. Most of the men I spoke with shared stories of faking that could just as easily have come from women: they were exhausted and ready for it to be over; the sex was subpar, but they still felt pressure to perform; they were hoping to bring an early end to a nonconsensual experience. An interview the *Village Voice* conducted with a man identified as "Male 26-Year-Old Who Has Faked an Orgasm" echoes some of the sentiments I've heard from women who didn't always know how to bring up their sexual quirks with a new or more casual partner. He says, "You could go out on a limb and say, 'I'm not going to bust until you start whistling Old Dixie while I read last week's *Economist* during the handjob so furiously fast and intense it begins to chafe your hand more than it does my dick,' but if you have some requirement to get off and yet don't feel comfortable putting it out there," faking becomes an easy way to keep everyone happy. (Though I did come across one uniquely male reason for faking it: two different men told me stories of hiding episodes of premature ejaculation by continuing the sexual encounter and offering up a fake orgasm later in the session, at a time deemed more appropriate.)

If men are faking orgasms, and doing it for reasons similar to their female counterparts, why is faking it so strongly associated with women? Some of this is doubtless a numbers game: women still cop to faking it at roughly double the rate of men. And those numbers don't factor in the frequency of faking it, making it possible that the total sum of faked female orgasms is much more than double that of faked male ones.

But it's also possible that our fixation with female fakery isn't just because it's a more frequent phenomenon. Maybe it's also related to the way the female body itself is treated as a unique object of fascination, fixation, objectification, and interest—something readily apparent in the way we continue to depict sex between men and women on-screen.

"It would be really fascinating to be able to build a time machine and go back in time before the invention of porn and find out how often women either faked or magnified their orgasm," Charlie Glickman says to me. "How much of this is the result of measuring ourselves against porn? How would somebody have even known what to do before they saw it on screen?"

There's no question that fake orgasms predate the modern era of widely available, and easily accessible, pornography. Back in the 1950s William Masters interviewed sex workers who claimed fake orgasm wasn't just possible but in fact common, and it's likely other women were faking it long before anyone thought to document the phenomenon. (The 1933 film *Ecstasy* features Hedy Lamarr having a presumably simulated on-screen orgasm, suggesting that even in the early twentieth century, women were aware that the right facial expressions could convincingly suggest sexual pleasure.)

But even if porn didn't create the fake orgasm, it's hard to deny the role it currently plays in shaping our ideas about what sexual pleasure looks like. Sex education—particularly the pleasure-focused variety that doesn't shy away from graphic descriptions and depictions of bedroom activities—has never been a huge priority in American culture. And as access to pornography has become cheap, easy, and discreet, it's filled the vacuum left by substandard (or completely absent) sex education with fantasy versions of sex serving as the only erotic primary resources most people get access to.

But what, exactly, is porn teaching women? Are the over-the-top moans and theatrical vocalizations found in porn convincing women that their own pleasure is in need of enhancement? Does our increased exposure to porn cause us to mimic the sex we see on-screen—and if so, where did porn's idea of pleasure come from in the first place? I decided to take a trip to Porn Valley to find out.

CHAPTER TWO

Everybody's Doing It

IN FEBRUARY 2009, Cindy Gallop—a start-up founder and former advertising executive—took the stage at TED, a prestigious conference with a self-proclaimed mission of spreading ideas. Gallop hadn't rehearsed her speech with the TED team—"TED had no idea what I was actually going to say," she tells me—and though she was aware that the conference had the beginnings of a web presence, and that her talk was being videotaped, she didn't expect her message to reach beyond the audience before her. "As far as I was concerned, I was only speaking to the people in the room," she says.

Standing on the TED stage, the then forty-nine-year-old Gallop cut a striking figure. With an angular blond bob, tight black pants, and stiletto boots, she's a far cry from the stereotypical vision of a woman on the edge of fifty—and as soon as she starts to speak, it's clear that her talk is not what the audience was expecting.

"I date younger men," Gallop's talk begins. "Predominantly men in their twenties. And when I date younger men, I have sex with younger men. And when I have sex with younger men, I encounter very directly and personally the real ramifications of the creeping ubiquity of hardcore pornography in our culture."

Over the course of four minutes, Gallop goes on to outline those "real ramifications." In the absence of solid sex education and frank discussion of sexuality, she tells the audience, pornography has become the default sex ed vehicle for millennials, and both men and women grow up thinking that the acts they witness in pornographic films—ubiquitous facials, anal sex, and rough blow jobs, for starters—are the be-all and end-all of what sexual intimacy can entail.

"Because the porn industry is driven by men, funded by men, managed by men, directed by men, and targeted at men, porn tends to present one worldview," Gallop continues. "Porn says, 'This is the way it is,' and what I want to say is, 'Not necessarily.'"

Gallop's talk struck a chord, both with the TED audience and the world beyond. When video of her presentation was posted on YouTube months later, it racked up over a million views; subsequently, Gallop launched MakeLoveNotPorn.tv, her own hardcore porn site pitched as a remedy to the failings of the adult industry. Where porn offered up fantasy, MakeLoveNotPorn would offer reality—or, in Gallop's hashtag-heavy parlance, #realworldsex.

The MakeLoveNotPorn argument is an appealingly simple one: Young people, bereft of any information about what sex is supposed to be like, turn to the internet and find their way to internet porn, which serves up a uniform and inaccurate vision of intimacy that imprints upon their impressionable, developing brains. When they eventually enter a sexual relationship, the men act out what they've seen on-screen, the women pretend to like it, and no one actually winds up having any real fun at all.

But appealing, simple narratives aren't necessarily correct ones. So how much truth is there to Gallop's portrayal of American porn consumption? And is it the whole truth, or are there other factors? Where are women learning that there's a "right" way to be sexual, and why are we taking that message to heart?

Cindy Gallop didn't invent the idea that porn shapes—and potentially ruins—the way we think about and engage in pleasure and sex. Anti-pornography feminists have long considered that to be the case; in the years leading up to Gallop's talk, both Pamela Paul and Ariel Levy penned books that took the adult industry to task for its effect on the bedroom.[1]

But there are a few important differences between Gallop and her predecessors. Unlike critics like Paul, Gallop is emphatically *not* anti-porn, instead positioning herself as both pro-sex and pro-porn (and, just to hit her message home, "pro–knowing the difference"). Where past critics of porn have been perceived as fun-hating scolds and prudish censors, Gallop wants to be seen as an open-minded libertine who just also believes in education—more the fun aunt who equips you with condoms and birth control than the parent who insists that abstinence until marriage is the only way to go. That attitude has allowed her to critique the adult industry without getting written off as a buzzkill, and in combination with her marketing background, it enabled Gallop to package her message into something so appealing and concise that it quickly became embedded in the public consciousness.

In the years since Gallop's talk, the notion that porn is affecting our sex lives has more or less become accepted as

---

[1] *Pornified* and *Female Chauvinist Pigs*, respectively.

fact. Personal essays lamenting the lackluster sexual encounters of single young women automatically nod at porn as the obvious explanation for their plight. A *Time* magazine cover story from March 2016 declared the medium to be a "threat to virility." Even the Republican Party has gotten in on the action, declaring adult media to be a "public health crisis" in their 2016 national platform (language that's also been used by a handful of state lawmakers).

So what, exactly, is porn supposedly teaching us about sex? Gallop's original talk was peppered with mentions of X-rated acts—facials, anal sex, spitting, dirty talk—that she declared were much more popular in porn than they were with civilian women. But to assume that she's merely on a crusade against facials is to miss her larger point.

Eight years after her TED talk, I am sitting in Gallop's midtown triplex, drinking tea as I listen to her hold forth on her beef with the adult industry. It's not actually about any sex act in particular, she explains; what truly bothers her is the way that porn—an industry unquestionably dominated by men—serves up a vision of sex that caters to a very particular, and very male, viewpoint.

The sexual landscape put forth by porn, Gallop argues, takes a few things to be gospel. First and foremost, sex is primarily about male pleasure, with women's pleasure and orgasm treated as secondary to the main event. Second, male pleasure is defined in purely penis-centric terms, with blow jobs and penetrative sex assumed to be the main items on the menu. And, finally, to the extent that female pleasure is ever factored in, it's presumed to be derived from the penis as well, with clitoris-stimulating activities like cunnilingus a taboo act.

It's not particularly controversial to note that these one-sided ideas about sex are fairly common. Indeed, a substantial chunk of pro-sex feminism is about advocating for a woman's right to pleasure in the bedroom. But is Gallop correct that today's young people are more likely to limit their sexual encounters to formulaic, often unsatisfying sexual scenarios? And if they are, is it solely due to the popularity of internet porn?

"It's really hard for me to separate how much of this is porn's fault versus how much is assumed to be porn's fault," Heather Corinna tells me over the phone. As the founder of the popular sex education site Scarleteen, Corinna has spent the past two decades chatting with young people about their sex lives; if anyone is well positioned to observe the effects of pornography on the developing young minds of America, it's her. But unlike Gallop, Corinna isn't convinced that porn is ruining sex—or even that porn, on its own, has created some monolithic idea of what sex is supposed to be.

Corinna isn't a porn apologist. She certainly recognizes that there are aspects of commercial pornography that promote less than healthy messages about human sexuality, and doesn't deny that porn consumption can influence our ideas about how to have sex.[2] But the narrative peddled by Gallop, which argues that sex was one way prior to the explosion of internet pornography and a different way now, strikes her as far too simplistic.

This sentiment was echoed by Tristan Taormino, a sex educator and feminist pornographer specializing in films that

---

[2] Corinna noted that, perhaps ironically, the very population that Gallop decries as being ruined by porn—twenty-something men interested in pursuing casual sex with women two or more decades their senior—is, in a way, a creation of porn itself. Were it not for the adult industry's fetishization of "cougars" and "MILFs," would women like Gallop be regularly sharing their beds with young men who were raised on porn in the first place?

offer up sex education and challenge the established norms of pornography that Gallop rails against. Like Corinna, Taormino spent the past two decades chatting with young people about their views on sex—though where Corinna connects to teens through message boards and chat programs, Taormino chats with college students in on-campus talks and workshops.

And if porn is dramatically influencing these young people in negative ways, Taormino isn't seeing it. At her workshops, she encourages attendees to submit anonymous questions about sex; as her student base has shifted from the tail end of Gen X through the millennials and into the postmillennial digital natives currently populating college campuses, those questions haven't really changed that much. If easy access to internet porn has had an impact on young people, it's mostly in the form of broadening their awareness of the diversity of sexual experience. Taormino notes that questions about squirting, pegging, strap-ons, and even BDSM are much more common than they were at the beginning of her career.

But is porn some dominating force that shapes everything in the bedroom? It isn't, as far as Taormino can tell. "There's this notion out there in the world that [young people's] entire sex life is consumed by porn, but I don't feel like there are more questions about porn [than there used to be]," she tells me. "The core questions are really about how my body works, how do I talk to my partner about this, how do I get what I want, how do I become good in bed?" Or, in other words, the exact same questions college students were asking about sex way back in the nineties, when porn wasn't easily (and freely) accessed with just a few clicks on your phone.

So if porn isn't the transformative force described by Gallop, why are so many commentators convinced that it is? If sex hasn't been radically altered by increased access to adult content, why have we been so ready to buy in to the notion that all our erotic woes can be pinned on a handful of smut peddlers based in the San Fernando Valley?

Well, for starters, porn is an easy target.

It's not merely that, as a fringe and still rather taboo industry, porn has few defenders (though it certainly is that in part). As an industry that traffics in explicit imagery, that caters to our most indecent urges and seediest curiosities,[3] porn is, in effect, the human id laid bare. Or, to be more accurate, the white, heterosexual male id laid bare: however much progress has been made in diversifying the industry behind the scenes (and, to be clear, quite a bit has been made), there's no question that the straight white male gaze is the dominant force within the most popular corners of the porn industry.

If you only dip a toe in the vast ocean that is pornography, it's easy to get the sense that it's all one very specific, potentially toxic product. All the messaging about sex and relationships that's subtly winked at in our culture is dialed up to eleven within pornography, taken to an extreme and explicit conclusion. Porn doesn't merely hint at the idea of women as objects created to sexually service men; it blatantly states it, with titles that emphatically reduce women[4]

---

[3] But not, necessarily, the desires we're looking to explore in our own bedrooms: what's often forgotten in discussions of porn is that many people are interested in films that depict scenarios they aren't capable of, or aren't interested in, engaging in in real life.

[4] Or, in the case of the much less discussed gay porn, men.

to a collection of body parts and attributes.[5] Minus the window dressing of manners and metaphor, porn makes it hard to ignore the ugliness of some of our most deeply held prejudices and beliefs—and it's not hard to see why some would be inclined to blame the messenger rather than critique the underlying message.

Additionally, the most popular—or at least most easily accessed—genres of internet porn tend to adhere to a rather predictable point of view and notion of what sexy looks like. Some of this is a result of the same factors that encourage homogeneity in TV, film, and music—white men have money, white men pay to produce art, the art that results caters to the desires of those white men—but it's also a product of what Gallop refers to as porn's "self-perpetuated categorization system." In order to find porn, you have to know the name of the thing you want to see; if no one's thought to label, say, men having sex in hiking boots as its own specific genre, then it's likely going to be harder for you to find it. And if you can't find it and watch it, pornographers won't know that you want to see it in the first place—meaning that the triple-X terms originally introduced by the (again, white and male) powers that be in the adult industry get more and more popular over time, while niches they weren't aware of to begin with find it challenging to find a foothold.

Which isn't to say that it's impossible. Longtime porn performer Ela Darling explains to me that "most porn companies make porn based on search terms" and that there's a particular interest in genres and fetishes that are "being searched for [but aren't currently] provided." Indie success

---

[5] Titles from the nominees list for the 2018 AVN Awards, aka the Oscars of porn, include *Big Wet Asses 26*, *Cum on My Tattoo*, *Black Squirters*, *Latin Asses 3*, and *Cougar Creampie*, just to name a few.

stories like the punk-rock Burning Angel and queer Crash Pad Series offer solid proof that, provided with evidence of consumer interest, the adult industry is more than happy to update its vision of what's sexy. Prior to Burning Angel, heavily tattooed women were considered a consumer turn-off by major studios like Vivid and Hustler; just over a decade after Burning Angel's launch, the inked-all-over Bonnie Rotten won the coveted Female Performer of the Year award from *AVN*, one of the adult industry's biggest trade publications. Similarly, the Crash Pad Series has demonstrated that authentic depictions of queer sex, and bodies that bend or break the gender binary, do, in fact, attract a paying audience—and, in response, mainstream directors like Dana Vespoli have released films that cater to this crowd.

But even as the landscape of the adult industry shifts and diversifies, many people aren't actually looking for, or finding, anything that exists outside the classic vision of porn, one where the breasts are large, the facials are frequent, and male pleasure is the primary priority. Porn consumption is still highly stigmatized—sure, we all know everyone looks at it, but if you're actually devoting time to finding exactly the video you want, or doing a deep dive into the overwhelming abundance of porn genres, there's a lingering assumption that there might be something wrong with you.

In the absence of a comprehensive examination of every available porn genre, many people wind up assuming that the first movie that pops up when they do a Google search for "porn" is a comprehensive representative of everything that's available—even when it's indicative of nothing more than the fantasy of one particular director who happens to have found mass appeal. Corinna compares the front page of a site like PornHub to the selection at an airport bookstore or grocery store book rack; for Darling, Top 40 radio feels like an apt comparison. "If you're not making the effort to explore what's [available in the world of porn or music], then of course you're going to have a very narrow view of what that industry is," Darling tells me. "But that's not anyone's fault but your own."

And if the problem is more about the porn that's being *found* than the porn that's being *made*, that would suggest that there's some factor at play aside from whatever's going down in the studios of Porn Valley. Particularly since, as Corinna tells me, the long-standing suspicion our culture has of porn—which precedes MakeLoveNotPorn by quite a bit—means that "there are more people right now walking into porn ready to be at least a little critical," to recognize the fake, staged, or other fantastical elements and separate them from what's real. That's not necessarily true for the other forces that shape our sex lives.

In theory, I'm the target audience for Gallop's message. I'm a millennial woman, one with a fair amount of experience dating young men who grew up in the porn-rich and sex-education-poor environment derided by Gallop. In the very years when Gallop was effectively conducting field research for her TED talk, bedding twenty-something young men and analyzing their bedroom behavior, I was also having erotic adventures with a number of young men. But the experience of sex she describes—one where female orgasm takes a backseat to its male counterpart, where blow jobs are celebrated while cunnilingus is taboo—bears little resemblance to the sexual landscape that I came of age in.

If anything, the sexual techniques and attitudes that Gallop describes as inescapable are exactly the opposite of what I experienced during the exact same time frame, with the same demographic of men. Where Gallop bedded penis-focused paramours with no consideration for her orgasm—so different from the young men of her youth—I repeatedly encountered men for whom my orgasm was a central consideration, and the supposedly taboo cunnilingus one of the primary methods of attempting to achieve it.

Were these men somehow the rare few who managed to escape the influence of porn? Did they all happen to grow up with solid sex education that taught them to be skeptical of the teachings of the adult industry? Unlikely. If anything, chances are good that they were under the influence of another cultural touchstone: 2004's *She Comes First*, an instructional guide written by sex counselor Ian Kerner that educates men who have sex with women about the importance of female orgasm—specifically, female orgasm produced through cunnilingus.

If you subscribe to Gallop's worldview, a book like Kerner's should be a breath of fresh air. And indeed, for many people it was. *Cosmopolitan* lauded it as "every man's must-read," the *New York Times* declared it to be "the Encyclopaedia Britannica of the clitoris," and even the executive producer of *Sex and the City* popped up to declare the book to be "required reading for all men who are dating and all women who are wondering why they're not satisfied."

I would not be quite so generous in praising Kerner's debut book; to be honest, I wouldn't praise it at all. However noble Kerner's intentions, his manual served less to liberate women or improve heterosexual men's bedroom behavior than to set up a brand-new paradigm for what sexual experiences "should" be like. As Corinna puts it to me, "It's not empowering for women for a man to literally write a book where he literally in the title decides what happens with sex for women. From the fucking front, literally from the book cover: this is in fact the opposite of empowering for women. You are literally telling everyone, men and women alike, as a man, what happens in sex for women and what's the right thing."

Left out of the *She Comes First* narrative? Women who—for whatever reason—don't want their orgasm prioritized during sex, or don't want to, or can't, orgasm at all. Women who don't enjoy receiving oral sex, or for whom it's fun but not capable of inspiring orgasm. Women who don't enjoy direct clitoral stimulation. Women who, perhaps, want an orgasm that comes after a male partner's or who want to kick things off with penetration ("There's a time and a place for everything, and the time for intercourse is after she's experienced her first orgasm," Kerner writes). Honestly, the book leaves out any woman whose vision of a successful sexual experience happens to look in any way unlike the scenarios laid out by Kerner, who seems to have a difficult time conceiving of a woman who doesn't fit the mold of his book. When a reader notes that his girlfriend doesn't like oral sex because it hurts, Kerner automatically assumes it's an issue of technique rather than preference. "You may have been too rough, or overzealous," he says, refusing to entertain the possibility that some women just might not like oral sex, no matter how skillfully it happens to be performed.

Rather than encouraging young men to engage in conversation and learn how their female partners might want their night passion to unfold, Kerner merely arms them with a bunch of cunnilingual techniques and sends them on their way, convinced that they, and they alone, have the power to blow a woman's mind. The result wasn't pretty.

A sampling of cunnilingus-related advice from *Cosmopolitan* writer Frank Kobola[6] gives an indication of what sort of man Kerner unleashed on the world. Musing on the topic of women who just aren't into getting head, Kobola surmises that "maybe it's self-consciousness, a prior negative experience, or just ambivalence," before going on to implore these women to "please, give it another chance. Give it lots of chances. Give it every chance. When oral sex works, it's good. We just have to make it work."

We just have to make it work. Not "We have to figure out what makes sex enjoyable for you," or "We have to work together to create a mutually fulfilling sense of physical intimacy," but we have to make this one specific sexual act "work"—with "work," of course, implying that the act results in orgasm (though, to his credit, Kobola notes that it's fine if oral sex merely feels good but doesn't unleash the big O—as he notes, "There's a reason it's considered foreplay"[7]).

Sex with a man like Kobola can be an exhausting experience for a woman. When we meet at a coffee shop, Taormino tells me about her own encounters with this particular breed of paramour. "I've always thought it was because I'm queer, but I do sleep with cis men, and I feel like they're like, 'Okay, she's gotten really good head, I gotta step up to the plate,'" she begins. "And in my own sexuality and how I'm wired, that's fun for me, but it never leads to orgasm. Under any circumstances."

You might think that a forty-five-year-old woman, one who's made a living exploring her own sexuality and educating others about their own, could be trusted to know her

---

[6] Published in *Cosmopolitan* as "Cosmo Frank."

[7] I'm rolling my eyes right now. Can you sense me rolling my eyes?

own body and sexual response cycle. And yet that was not the case. According to Taormino, the response she got from these obstinate pussy eaters was more along the lines of, "I know you say that, but you don't know. I'm going to do it now, and I'm going to make you come that way." If it seems ironic that a male sexpert who claims to be on a mission to improve sex for women could ultimately create a situation where a female sexpert's sex life is, in fact, reduced in quality as her partner refuses to listen to her in favor of listening to another man—well, such is the irony of *She Comes First*.

"He's not slept with the guy that he's suggesting guys be or else he would know that nobody wants to fuck that guy," Corinna says of Kerner. His tract claiming to offer women a path to greater happiness ultimately positioned female orgasm—and orgasm unleashed through cunnilingus, at that—as a badge of honor and proof of a man's virility, rendering women's actual needs, desires, and authentic pleasure subordinate to the appeasement of the heterosexual male ego. It teaches men that—in Corinna's words—"all is lost if you don't have an orgasm," and the kind of sex that results isn't fun, intimate, or in any way good for women.

More significantly, Kerner's conviction that cunnilingus is the be-all and end-all of female sexual pleasure sets his acolytes up to believe that any woman who claims otherwise is lying, misinformed, or aggressively ignorant of her own sexual potential. In his mission to liberate women to experience greater sexual pleasure, Kerner traps an entire group of people in a rather narrow definition of intimacy—and positions men to assume that any woman who claims to exist outside that framework is not to be believed.

*   *   *

As much as I dislike *She Comes First*, I do not think the book itself, or Kerner specifically, is the root cause of anyone's sexual woes. Nor do I think that the vast and complex adult industry can really be held accountable for "ruining" sex. While it's true that both porn and *She Comes First* have provided impressionable young people with less than stellar guidance on how to conduct their sex lives, those effects are merely the symptoms of a much larger problem, one that predates pretty much any flick or tome that may have taught you how you're supposed to have sex—and that's the idea that there is one specific way that anyone is "supposed" to be having sex at all, or, as Darling puts it, "the greater holistic problem where everyone's expected to come in a certain way at a certain time."

It's a narrative that's nearly inescapable, one that makes its way into virtually every conversation about sex: in magazines, on TV, in the media's discussion of whatever "weird" sexual practice a politician has just been accused of. Before porn consumption, before we turn to the best-selling manuals penned by self-proclaimed sexperts, most of us have already embraced the idea that there is a normal, correct, or in any way universal way to have sex, and that if we can only unlock it, we'll be able to achieve the highest levels of sexual pleasure, in every sexual encounter, with every sexual partner we ever engage with. The specifics of the script may vary from source to source, but the idea that there *is* a script we should be following to begin with is widely accepted as fact.

While this narrative affects everyone of every gender and sexual orientation, it's particularly fixated on the sexual response of vulvae and vaginas—largely due to an assumption that they're far more mysterious and complex than the straightforward, easily understood penis.[8] The female orgasm is routinely positioned as one of the greatest medical mysteries around, one that, with enough scientific research, the sexological community will be able to unlock a universal formula for.

Sexperts throughout history have wound up championing their own particular visions of female sexual pleasure.[9] With every groundbreaking finding about the clitoris comes a trendy new script, one we're inevitably told is the one true path to orgasmic excellence. If it seems strange to think of something so ingrained as orgasm as the product of a fad, consider that it's no less weird than each decade being associated with, say, a particularly fashionable body type: a woman can no more transform herself from a voluptuous, big-breasted hourglass to a stick-thin twig than she can re-map her pleasure response from clitoris to G-spot, but our cultural narratives seem to suggest that—for the woman who wants to be with it—both of these impossibilities should be options, so long as you're willing to put in enough effort.

Freud, of course, was known for championing vaginal sexual pleasure over its "immature" clitoral counterpart; decades later, feminists like Anne Koedt declared the vaginal orgasm to be a "myth," championing a return to clitoral stimulation and pleasure. In the 1980s, the pendulum swung back toward

---

[8] It is, to put it bluntly, wildly inaccurate to position male sexuality as incredibly simple or entirely about the penis, but it's an assumption that persists even in spite of evidence that the prostate, nipples, and a variety of assorted other parts of the male anatomy can enhance and impact the male sexual response.

[9] Sometimes unintentionally, after their words and research get misunderstood postpublication.

internal stimulation with the publication of *The G Spot: And Other Recent Discoveries About Human Sexuality*, a work that popularized the idea that stimulating a section at the front of the vaginal canal could lead to intense sexual pleasure (and, potentially, female ejaculation). Vibrators, cunnilingus, and orgasmic meditation have all had their champions as well, each body part or sexual act served up by someone, somewhere, as the one true way to unlock the essential O. A chapter of Tim Ferriss's *The 4-Hour Body* is devoted to the DOing, or "deliberate orgasm," method, which promises unimaginable sexual ecstasy from fifteen minutes of applying light pressure to the allegedly hypersensitive upper-left quadrant of the clitoris.

There's nothing wrong with any of these methods of sexual stimulation: virtually all of them have been able to get *some* women to orgasm at some point in time, under some set of circumstances. The problem is our conviction that there's some sort of "natural" way for women to achieve orgasm—and that one specific method of achieving sexual pleasure somehow supersedes the actual interests and desires of any particular, individual woman.

Since the days of *The Hite Report*, a pioneering study of female sexual response published in 1976, feminists, avid cunnilinguists, and other supporters of putting clitoral stimulation front and center in discussions of female sexual pleasure have oft made note of the fact that a whopping 70 percent of women find themselves unable to orgasm from vaginal intercourse alone. Given that vaginal intercourse has historically been given primacy, it's a worthwhile point to raise: if over two-thirds of women can't orgasm from penile thrusting, it's probably worth reconsidering the idea that penis-in-vagina sex should be considered the primary path to female orgasmic bliss.

Yet at the same time, many clitoral advocates ignore the fact that the 30 percent of women who *can* orgasm from vaginal intercourse are not an insignificant portion of the population. In the rush to debunk the idea that all women should orgasm from one specific activity, we end up promoting the idea that all women should orgasm from another, different, yet no less specific activity, and we never seem to recognize the irony in this reversal. The problem isn't the method by which the majority of women can, or can't, come. The problem is trying to pleasure a sexual partner in a way that just doesn't work for them.

There's no one way to bring a person to sexual bliss, and all the statistics and numbers and approved techniques mean nothing when you're in bed with someone whose body and sexual response style don't line up with the platonic ideal of a sexual person. To offer an analogy from outside the realm of sex: we all know that while bacon may be a wildly popular food, it's unlikely to do you any favors if you're trying to win over one of the millions of Americans who happen to be vegetarian, vegan, Jewish, or Muslim. Yet even though we understand that different people have different likes and dislikes when it comes to food (or fashion or music or virtually any other aspect of life), we continue to buy into the idea that there's a "normal" way to get off, or that the pattern that works for the largest percentage of people is the one that we should all default to in bed.

Why are we so susceptible to every scientist, doctor, journalist, or self-proclaimed sexpert who claims to have mastered the art of the one true orgasm?

The most obvious reason is our country's lack of commitment to quality sex education—and to be sure, that deep and abiding problem is a major contributor to our misguided ideas about what sex can, and cannot, be. But to blithely throw out "sex education" as the cure-all for what ails us runs the risk of suggesting that merely tossing more money at condom and STI (sexually transmitted infection) education—the only sex education most schools are set up to provide—will fix everything, when the issue is a much deeper, and more fundamental, cultural problem.

Most of us are raised in environments where explicit discussion of sexuality is still considered taboo, where even the most progressive sex education is focused on preventing harm rather than increasing pleasure. The act of sex becomes something of a mystery box: we know its contents are important, that it allegedly holds the key to an eternity of fulfilling relationships and unending happiness—and, in our desperate search to achieve that ecstasy, we often fall victim to the first (or second or third) charlatan who claims that they've seen what lies within.

Our refusal as a culture to talk openly and honestly about the complexities of human sexual experience limits the impact of the sex education we do receive, and leaves us vulnerable to anyone unscrupulous enough to peddle the claim that they have the universal solution for mind-blowing sex. But even that isn't the whole of the problem. While we may not talk explicitly about sex, we frequently offer commentary on the act in indirect and opaque terms (think of all the suggestive advertising campaigns and sitcom double entendres you've been exposed to), burnishing the exterior of that metaphorical mystery box even as we refuse to open it.

This double whammy of taboo and hyperglorification creates an added incentive to fake it. If you've learned that your skill at sex will determine your desirability as a partner, but no one's explained that being good in bed is far more about empathy than any specific moves, then any model of "good sex" that you stumble across—whether it's in a porn flick, a steamy novel, or some hot new sexpert's handbook—can seem like a holy dictum rather than just one isolated example of how some people like to do it. And should you discover that the holy dictum leaves you more uncomfortable than aroused, it's easy to conclude that you're the one who's in the wrong and that your best option is to suck it up and play pretend, lest someone discover you're—gasp!—secretly bad at sex. Whether that means feigning a love of facials or gritting your teeth and bearing it while someone goes downtown doesn't really matter. What matters is that we've been taught to see other people as the authority on our own sexual desires.

In my conversations about pornography, everyone I spoke with—even Cindy Gallop—acknowledged that porn merely provides the finishing touches on a narrative of sex and relationships that most of us received well before our first porn experience. Porn might fill in the blanks of our sexual script with blow jobs and anal and facials, but the notion that the script itself exists, that it needs to be filled out in one specific way, is established somewhere else entirely.

According to Corinna, many young women—primarily, though not exclusively, straight young women—arrive at Scarleteen with a very specific mindset about how sex is supposed to play out, in broad strokes if not in detail. "They want to know how to meet X expectation, perform X thing, [and] meet the assumed male expectation that they're assuming guys will have," she tells me. Tellingly, this mindset is formed in the absence of any actual evidence that men truly do both want and expect one specific set of sexual acts.

Most of these young women haven't even had the chance to fail to live up to some mythical expectation, because these beliefs seem to be put in place before young women have any experience with sex.

In fact, it's hard to consider any one thing the original source for this belief, because wherever you go, you're guaranteed to find it. Magazines, romantic comedies, sitcoms, dating experts—virtually any mainstream source for answers or advice on the topics of sex and dating is almost guaranteed to reinforce the notion that there's a natural, and right, way for our romantic and sexual relationships to unfold. And even when you're as far away as you can possibly get from pornography—like, say, in a chaste, woman-friendly rom com—you're still likely to run into the exact same assumptions that shape and restrict mainstream porn, albeit in a significantly tamer fashion.

"If you surveyed a group of seven-year-old girls and asked them things about what happens on a date, for example, I think they could fill in a lot of information," Taormino says. "I bet that they would give you a basic romantic comedy sort of narrative." Boy asks girl out, boy picks girl up, boy pays for date, boy initiates the good night kiss and any other physically intimate acts—the male-led romance narrative is so ingrained into our culture that most of us barely think to question it. Women who "act like men" and take the lead in sex and relationships, and do so in a way that's not treated as problematic by the narrative, are still so rare that when Taormino and I tried to think of a pop culture example, the main one that came to mind was *Sex and the City*'s Samantha Jones, a character created a full two decades ago.

Which isn't to say that the male-led narrative of sex and dating that pops up in most movies, TV, music, literature, and, yes, porn is in and of itself the problem. As the unintentionally oppressive *She Comes First* made clear, swapping a male-focused pleasure narrative for a female-focused one only counts as progress if you happen to be fulfilled by the narrow dictates laid out by that narrative. It's the idea that there is one "normal" way of finding happiness in our bedrooms and our relationships—that it's a real and achievable thing, and not a statistical fiction—that puts us in a bind. The notion that there's a single, universal answer to the question of what women (and men) want traps us in an uncomfortable position.

Until we're able to embrace the radical idea that there are many different ways of achieving pleasure and fulfillment, that each and every one of us must figure out for ourselves what exactly works for us, women who don't fit the mold established by society have two ways forward. They can be true to themselves and deal with the fallout of not fitting in—partners who can't understand or won't go along with their genuine desires, friends and family who insist they can't possibly be happy with the choices they've made—or betray their own truth by superficially adapting to adhere to the expectations laid out by society. The latter, not surprisingly, is the path of least resistance.

The third slide in Gallop's original MakeLoveNotPorn presentation declares that in the porn world, "women come *all* the time in positions where nothing is going on anywhere *near* the clit," meaning, of course, that porn performers frequently give the impression that they're orgasming from penetrative intercourse alone—and, presumably, that young people have bought into this idea. But Corinna still remains skeptical that anyone—even the most porn-obsessed young person—is still laboring under the belief that intercourse guarantees orgasm for everyone. "1998 called, it wants its sex information back," she jokes, going on to say that even the fourteen-year-olds who visit Scarleteen are well aware that penis-in-vagina stimulation is likely to be better for the penis than for the vagina. "They might not like that fact, they might come in asking how can they not live that reality, but they know it."

But if young people are well aware that intercourse-induced orgasms aren't incredibly common, why is there so much emphasis on achieving them? Why are vaginal orgasms—to use Corinna's term—the "golden fleece" for the young men she counsels?

Perhaps because of the elevated status that vaginal intercourse holds in our pantheon of sexual activity. For reasons both logical (like its role in procreation) and debatable (such as its relative intimacy when compared to other sexual acts), putting a penis in a vagina is still viewed as the be-all and end-all of sexual intimacy. It's the act we're most likely to think of when someone says they had sex—no qualifier needed as with anal or oral or any other variation. It's the act that's considered "all the way," while sex with fingers or tongues or toys might still be considered half measures. And, perhaps most significantly of all, it's the one act universally considered to have a transformative effect on a person—and, in particular, a woman—the first time they engage in it.

Yes, I'm referring to virginity and the supposedly life-changing milestone that is "losing" it. Most of us grow up believing that virginity is something real, measurable, and probably correlated with a penis forcing its way into a vagina and demolishing a hymen—yet that may be one of the most long-standing cultural fictions that force women to fake it.

CHAPTER THREE

I'm a Virgin

AS A YOUNG girl, Mona Eltahawy was raised to understand the importance of her purity. "I don't think anyone said the word 'virginity' outright, but it was understood, and I was taught—by my family, through religious studies, at school, through the culture I grew up in—that I would not be having sex until I got married." Even in a relatively progressive home, where Eltahawy was taught about the reproductive mechanics of sex at the age of nine, there was no question that premarital sex was absolutely unacceptable.

It was a message that Eltahawy—who spent her adolescence in the United Kingdom and Saudi Arabia, moving back to Egypt in her twenties—took seriously. "For me, the mere thought of having sex before I got married just terrified me. I was your typical 'good girl,'" a status reinforced by her decision, at the age of sixteen, to voluntarily don a hijab. "That also helped keep the flag flying for virginity," she tells me. "I couldn't conceive of being a woman in hijab who then had sex before marriage."

There was just one problem: Eltahawy didn't want to get married, and she had no desire to have children. "I was having panic attacks at the age of seventeen where I would have a nightmare and wake up in a panic that I had married the wrong man," she tells me. Unwilling to have sex before marriage, but equally unwilling to settle down and start a family, she decided to ignore relationships and focus on her career.[1] "I was totally, passionately, consumed by journalism.... I was doing really well in my journalism career, and not even thinking about relationships or sex."

Eltahawy eventually got tired of being a "good girl." She got tired of staying pure. In her mid-twenties, she took off her hijab, a garment she'd been wearing mostly because of pressure from the community around her. A few years later, she found a man she liked and was attracted to, and—despite what she'd been taught about sex outside of marriage—she began exploring everything she'd been told to save for marriage. And at twenty-nine, she decided to experience the act she'd been told would ruin the rest of her life. It was, she tells me, wonderful.

It was also a bit isolating. "It took me forever to be able to talk to anyone about my first experience with intercourse," she says. "I was really worried about being judged." In the late 1990s, Egyptian and Muslim women rarely spoke openly about sex; initially, Eltahawy only talked about her sex life with friends who came from outside of those communities. But as time went on, she felt increasingly that it was important to spark a conversation about sex with other Muslim women. At a feminist conference for Muslim women in Kuala Lumpur, Eltahawy spoke publicly about her decision to have sex as an unmarried woman. The response was exactly as she'd feared: "No one gave me a reciprocal experience. They just listened." One woman went so far as to quote the Qu'ran, telling Eltahawy, "'The pure are for the

---

[1] And, for what it's worth, started masturbating a lot. "From the age of eleven onwards, I was able to make myself come just fine," she tells me—which made it vastly easier for her to wait.

pure, and the impure are for the impure,' so you'll find someone who also fornicated."

The purity obsession that pervaded Eltahawy's youth defines the lives of many women in the Middle East, dotting their days with consequences that range from mild inconvenience to traumatic, potentially life-threatening horror. In Egypt, she tells me, tampons are relatively unpopular; a fear of damaging the hymen and being rendered impure leads many women to rely on pads alone. A similar reverence for the hymen compromises the gynecological care provided to unmarried women. In a misguided attempt to preserve their patients' purity, doctors refrain from performing internal vaginal exams on unmarried women. Once, when Eltahawy developed a yeast infection, her physician diagnosed her based on her reported symptoms alone.

In the most extreme cases, the fixation on the preservation of the hymen can lead to the violation of a woman's bodily autonomy, and even the mutilation of her sexual anatomy. After the Arab Spring protests in Tahrir Square, unmarried women were subjected to "virginity tests," which more or less amounted to sexual assault at the hands of a doctor—an action the military attempted to justify by noting that the protesters weren't "good girls" and therefore their bodily autonomy could be considered forfeit. "They were saying this knowing that what they did would be accepted by society at large, because society at large believes it can subject women to so-called virginity tests," Eltahawy explains, noting that many women are forced to secure "proof" of virginity from a doctor before getting married.

Even female genital mutilation—a horrific procedure that ranges from the removal of part, or all, of the clitoris to the wholesale cutting and repositioning of the labia with the intent to create a vaginal seal—is often framed as a way of keeping young women "intact."

When the pressure to remain "pure" is so incredibly high, is it any surprise that some women might find a way to fudge it? In communities where purity culture is deeply ingrained, women not infrequently turn to artificial hymens or doctors who promise hymen reconstruction[2] that'll convince their new husbands they've never had sex—or, in some cases, make actually virginal vaginas more readily adhere to the expected form and function of an unpenetrated vagina.

In America, where pop culture is more likely to present virginity as a burden than a virtue, the stories Eltahawy documents in her book *Headscarves and Hymens: Why the Middle East Needs a Sexual Revolution* can seem otherworldly—more an indication of particular regions' backward attitudes toward women and sex than an extreme manifestation of a universal fixation on female purity. Yet to assume that Americans are above building a shrine to the intact hymen is to ignore America's own love affair with purity—or, as it's often called, abstinence until marriage.

Americans may package our virginity obsession somewhat differently than the Egyptians do, but that doesn't mean it's nonexistent. Purity balls and promise rings are fairly well-documented phenomena, but they're only the tip of the iceberg. Hymen reconstruction, though less common than in the Middle East, is performed at clinics like

---

[2] How frequently do women seek out refurbished hymens? Because of the understandably secretive nature of this request, it's difficult to properly assess, but a 2010 survey of Swedish health care providers gives some indication. Of the 507 providers who responded to the questionnaire, 271 had seen patients requesting what the paper terms "virginity-related care."

Ridgewood Health and Beauty Center in Queens, New York (which makes no bones about what sort of "health and beauty" it's about—the practice's website, hymenridgewood surgery.com, proudly declares RHBC to be "the pioneer of hymenoplasty"). Virginity tests also take place on our shores: In October 2015, newlywed Brelyn Bowman began popping up in the media after a photo from her wedding went viral on social media. The photo itself wasn't particularly remarkable—just Bowman dancing with her father, Pastor Mike Freeman—but in the caption, Bowman noted that "I was able to present a certificate of purity to [Freeman] signed by my doctor that my hymen was still intact," a claim that inspired a great deal of public interest. As Bowman's photo exploded with likes and comments, its backstory began making the rounds in the press. In her teen years, Bowman had signed a covenant pledging to maintain her virginity until marriage; the purity certificate was merely a culmination of that pledge. Purity certificates were something of a Freeman family tradition: Bowman's older sister had presented their father with one at her own wedding, six years before.[3]

In what may be the most American take on hymen worship, a number of young women have made headlines by putting their virginity up for auction, racking up impressive sums from men vying for the right to be first penis in. In the spring of 2014, a medical student using the name Elizabeth Raine threw her own V-card onto the market,[4] backing up her claims to purity by noting that "I am able to prove my

---

[3] Notably, Bowman's brother—who'd also signed a purity pledge for their father— engaged in premarital sex and did not have a purity certificate of his own.

[4] And later pulled it back off, announcing her decision to cancel the auction after receiving a bid of $801,000.

virginity by medical examination" and that "upon request I will submit myself for unbiased physical examination and/or polygraph testing."

Modern Americans may not always ostracize women for engaging in premarital sex, but we still see female virginity as something that carries an inherent worth (in the case of women like Raine, a literal as well as figurative one), particularly if you can "prove" it. That belief puts an incredible amount of pressure on women—to stay pure, to make their first time "worth it," to bleed during their first sexual encounter lest their partner suspect dishonesty—that's all the more tragic given that our whole conception of virginity is largely based on a myth.

In the classic framing of virginity, everything is clear and simple. You're a virgin until you're not, and the act that moves you from one camp into the other leaves you forever transformed in both body and spirit. A penis penetrates a vagina, a hymen is disposed of, a girl becomes a woman, and innocence is supplanted by a worldly maturity. But what if it's not so simple? What if virginity isn't a physical condition that manifests itself in the body? What if it isn't even a discrete, definable social rite of passage? If virginity is more a state of mind—and a vague one at that—then why have we invested so much time and energy into convincing women that it matters? Why has so much time and energy been invested into crafting methods to determine whether or not women are faking their sexual innocence—and why are we convinced that vaginal virginity can be proven at all?

For centuries, men have devoted countless hours to devising methods for figuring out how to determine whether women are lying about their virginity. But perhaps a better question is this: What does it mean to tell the truth?

*   *   *

Ashley isn't quite sure when, exactly, she lost her virginity.

It's not that she doesn't remember the first time a penis entered her vagina, or that she's hazy on the details of her earliest sexual experiences. When we chat, she's able to recount a number of early sexual encounters—ones that affected her deeply, ones that left her underwhelmed—it's just that she's not quite sure which one "counts."

Like many other women, Ashley began exploring her sexuality in her mid-teens, making out with her high school boyfriend and experimenting with a variety of nonpenetrative sexual pleasures (like the age-old classic dry humping—or, if you prefer, "grinding"). At seventeen, she began exploring oral sex; a year later, she had her first experience with penis-in-vagina penetration.

In a traditional narrative, that first moment of penile penetration would conclusively bring an end to Ashley's status as a virgin—but for Ashley, the experience wasn't that straightforward. For starters, that initial act of penetration was accidental—"He slipped in," she tells me—and brief, her partner pulling out almost as quickly as he'd entered her. It wasn't until her next relationship that Ashley had a full-fledged experience of vaginal intercourse to completion, and while that seemed to put the whole virginity question to rest, a few years later she found her entire narrative of sexual indoctrination thrown into upheaval all over again.

What sparked her renewed confusion? In her late twenties, Ashley began exploring sex with other women and, as a result, found herself reevaluating how important being penetrated by a penis was to her sexual identity in the first place. If her sexual experiences with women—which, in many cases, closely resembled some of the early explorations she'd enjoyed with her first boyfriend—were just as fulfilling as vaginal intercourse, did that mean she'd punched her V-card back when she was seventeen? And if those oral sex experiences *had* signaled the loss of her virginity, why hadn't they felt more transformative at the time?

Ashley's story is a familiar one to me, on both a personal and a professional level. At seventeen I sat in my college health center, unsure of whether or not to check a box indicating I had been sexually active, unsure of whether or not the experiences I'd had "counted." And over the years, I've come into contact with a number of women for whom virginity loss felt more like a spectrum of experiences than a specific turning point: women who spent days, or weeks, playing a game of "just the tip"; women whose initial sexual experiences were nonconsensual; women who had sex with women long before they ever explored their attractions to men—if they ever had sex with men at all. While there are certainly women whose sexual histories progressed down the socially ordained, conventionally heterosexual path, where kissing leads to groping leads to oral sex and then, in the grand finale of sexual maturity, penis-in-vagina intercourse, there are many, many women whose experiences exist outside that narrowly defined idea of "normal."

When I ask Ashley to locate a moment in her early sexual history that felt transformative—a sort of "point of no return," a moment after which everything felt different—she doesn't mention any of the experiences traditionally associated with virginity loss. No, her true moment of sexual awakening was something entirely different: her first orgasm, which occurred when she was fifteen and rubbing on her boyfriend. "I didn't know what it was, but I wanted to experience it again and began experimenting with him and on my own to duplicate the experience," she tells me. Yet as powerful as that initial orgasm was, she hesitates to call that her loss of virginity. "To me, there has to be some decision to have sex," she says.

Ashley's struggle to pinpoint her moment of virginity loss isn't a surprise to me—after all, virginity was never meant to encompass the breadth of modern sexual experience. A remnant of a time when women were chattel and men craved a way to ensure their bride's offspring had really sprung from their own loins, the concept doesn't neatly adapt to encompass queer sexualities, or even sex between a man and a woman that extends beyond the standard penis-in-vagina sort. Frankly, virginity strains to reflect the reality of women's bodies to begin with, and that may be its biggest problem of all.

At this point, I need to let you know something: the hymen isn't real.

I don't mean that the hymen isn't a reliable indicator of virginity, or that its presence or absence tells an observer absolutely nothing about someone's sexual history. Nor do I mean that—as many have noted before me—the hymen is often damaged or done away with by activities that have nothing to do with sex, like gymnastics or horseback riding or taking a particularly nasty fall. Or rather, I do mean all of that, but only as a subset of a larger, more important truth: the hymen, as it is popularly conceived, is a complete and utter work of fiction.

Most of us come of age with a vague notion that vaginas are naturally packaged with a thin flesh barrier, one that must be disposed of before sex can be properly enjoyed. And while the more progressive members of society are often aware that the hymen's reputation for indicating purity is wildly overblown, even they tend to buy into the idea that it exists—that vaginas are created impenetrable, that the vaginal opening must be forcibly forged, that successfully achieving first-time sex requires a payment of blood, flesh, and pain (even if that toll is ultimately paid, not to a pioneering penis, but to a tampon, horseback, or an enthusiastic split).

But to the extent that the hymen can be considered an identifiable part of the body, it's more as a by-product than an intentionally designed human seal of purity. In her book *Virgin: The Untouched History*, Hanne Blank describes the hymen as "a functionless leftover," noting that "in the simplest terms possible, a hymen is what's left over when you dig a hole." As the fetal vagina is hollowed out, the creation of the vaginal opening leaves some residue in its wake; that residue is what becomes the hymen. More decorative trim than functional organ, the hymen comes in a variety of shapes, sizes, and textures. Some hymens are fragile wisps that disintegrate at the slightest touch; others are stretchy, elastic, and capable of surviving well past the point of virginity loss.[5] There's no universal form or function to the bit of flesh that gets called the hymen, and there's certainly no vaginal seal of freshness waiting to be eradicated before first sex.

And yet despite its humble beginnings, the hymen has managed to amass a degree of power rivaling that of the body's most essential organs. There are few body parts quite so capable of completely, utterly altering the course of a woman's destiny—a pretty stunning achievement for

---

[5] Seriously. In *Virgin*, Blank writes of a woman whose "thick, very resilient septate hymen" was discovered during labor and had to be cut to allow for a successful delivery.

something that Therese Shechter, director of the documentary *How to Lose Your Virginity*, describes to me as "a membrane with a really good publicity agent."

How did such an insignificant bit of bodily tissue become the measure of a woman's worth? To a large degree, it was a cultural obsession with female virginity that created the hymen—or at least, elevated its status—and not the reverse. Long before a sixteenth-century Flemish anatomist named Andreas Vesalius "discovered"[6] the hymen, men had been busying themselves with devising increasingly creative ways to determine whether a woman might be impure (including, but not limited to, comparing the circumference of a woman's neck to the distance between the tip of her nose and the base of her skull). Virginity was an undetectable, ephemeral quality men desperately wanted a way to quantify; the hymen gained its elevated status by providing a somewhat plausible method of detection. As Blank writes in *Virgin*, "we became aware of hymens because we are aware of something called virginity. We found the hymen because we found reasons to search women's bodies for some bit of flesh that embodied this quality we call 'virginity,' some physical proof that it existed."

The impact of our belief in the hymen cannot be understated. At a fundamental level, it creates a situation where women are raised with an understanding of their intimate anatomy that simply isn't true—a degree of cognitive dissonance that can get particularly nasty when you're told your untouched genitals "prove" you've been having sex you've never actually engaged in. From the initial falsehood of the

---

[6] How did he "discover" it? By dissecting the corpses of two women he felt fairly certain were virgins: a nun and a teenage hunchback whom Vesalius deemed too ugly to be fuckable.

hymen comes a cascade of other erroneous, and often damaging, beliefs. If you believe that the hymen exists, you believe that virginity can be detected, and that it's possible—if
horrific—to create a sort of surveillance state around the
issue of female purity. If you believe that the hymen must
be vanquished before sex can be enjoyed, you believe that
a woman must experience pain and bleeding—even if it's
brought on by a tampon or a rough horseback ride—before
she can experience sexual pleasure. If you believe that a
woman must experience pain and bleeding during sex,
you've both normalized and created the expectation of painful first-time sex—leading women to believe that the discomfort or distress they feel during penis-in-vagina intercourse is
not merely normal but necessary and that if it doesn't hurt
or result in blood, they're somehow doing something wrong.

And many people do believe first-time penis-in-vagina
intercourse requires both pain and bloodshed—next to the
"intact" and presumably visible hymen, bleeding during sex
may be the most popular "proof" of virginity (or, at least, virginity newly vanquished). The notion is so normalized that
any woman who *doesn't* feel pain or bleed, who has fully enjoyable intercourse the first time around, is often presumed to
be lying, broken, or abnormal. A question featured on Columbia University's health Q & A site Go Ask Alice! encapsulates
this phenomenon, as a man who's recently enjoyed his first
sexual experience frets that his partner might be more experienced than she claims: "She didn't seem to be in any pain,
there was no bleeding, and there was no hymen. She makes
up all these excuses like 'not all girls have them.' Should I
believe her?"

The experts at Go Ask Alice! assure him that yes, he
should believe his partner, which, of course, they're correct

to do. The idea that blood and pain are an inherent part of first-time sex is specious at best. It's possible to experience first-time intercourse without the slightest bit of discomfort or bleeding (as, indeed, was Eltahawy's experience). Conversely, sexually experienced women can, and do, bleed and feel pain during intercourse, even if they've had enjoyable, pain-free sex a number of times before. Whether a vagina bleeds might have less to do with experience and anatomy than mechanics of the sex act itself: vaginal tissue is rather delicate; if it's not properly prepared for impact, then tearing and bleeding are a possibility. If a vagina's not properly lubricated—which might happen because an intercourse haver's not all that turned on, or because she's postmenopausal, or because she's dehydrated, or because her body just doesn't naturally create a lot of lube—then pain and bleeding can definitely occur; likewise if a vagina's too tensed up to easily allow penetration.

When I meet up with film director Shechter, she offers a theory for how the myth of the bloody hymen might have come into existence. It's not hard to imagine that a young woman with little in the way of sexual education might be terrified at the thought of letting a penis penetrate her; that fear alone can create the tension and lack of lubrication required to create those apocryphal signs of virginity loss. And since men haven't historically put a great deal of emphasis on ensuring their partners' pleasure, it's doubtful that sex in the age of Vesalius involved much of the foreplay that might prevent pain and bleeding from occurring.

From there it becomes a self-fulfilling prophecy: terrified women have sex with careless men, which leads to pain and bleeding; pain and bleeding become synonymous with first-time sex, which further terrifies women and leads men to

be careless about causing their partners pain. Once that expectation is in place, it neatly replicates itself. A belief that
first-time vaginal sex is "supposed" to hurt means that painful sex isn't seen as a problem, but rather a rite of passage
that women must suffer through[7]—and, by extension, that
women who actually enjoy their inaugural experience of
vaginal sex are somehow suspect.

Because of the myth of the hymen, it's not enough to honestly admit that you've never been vaginally penetrated:
you need to provide evidence in the form of blood and pain.
For women with purity-obsessed partners, that can mean
resorting to extreme measures—artificial hymens, stitched-
up vulvae, and fake cries of pain—all to ensure that everything goes as expected, *even if it truly is your first time*. When
you're asked to conform to a standard that has no basis in
reality, is it lying if you "cheat" to "prove" something that's
technically true? What if the lie is less about the mythical physical signs of virginity and more about the bizarre
cultural narrative we have about how first-time sex is "supposed" to happen?

My own virginity always seemed like something that mat-
tered more to other people than it did to me. A post–high
school fling told me upfront that he would not be putting his
penis in my vagina because I deserved to save that experience for someone more special than he was—a statement
that seemed odd both in its presumption of my own sexual
willingness and for the immediate limitations it placed on
the future of our relationship. When I started having sex in

---

[7] It should be noted here that some vaginas will bleed or hurt no matter how gentle a partner is—everyone's body is different, and it's impossible to predict how a
vagina will respond to a first-time experience of penetration.

college, I was loathe to disclose my relative innocence to any of my partners: a girlfriend discovered she was my first during a round of the drinking game "I Never," when a mutual friend instructed her to drink along with everyone else who'd punched the V-card of someone in that room.

But at twenty, sitting on the subway listening to my friends share the stories of their first times, I felt a twinge of discomfort, a sense that I had done it wrong somehow. My complex, multistage process of "losing it"—one that involved as much confusion, discomfort, and heartbreak as it did romance and pleasure—didn't fit the prepackaged story I'd grown up with about how to lose your virginity. And even among friends, sharing the full story of how it had happened to me felt a bit like admitting that something about me was inherently flawed and broken.

"One of the things that I have noticed in my years spent reading virginity-loss narratives is, if you've read one, you've read 'em all," Hanne Blank tells me. When she heard that a colleague had edited a collection of virginity-loss narratives, "I was like, 'You could have saved yourself a lot of time and just printed the same one out fifty times. They're all basically the same.'" The way we narrate our stories of virginity loss, Blank offers, is "uncommonly uniform," so much so that it's hard to believe that everyone is telling the truth—that we're not, perhaps, fudging some details to make our stories conform to a universally agreed-on societal norm.

Blank—who, as the author of a book about the history of virginity, has been asked to share her personal story more times than she can count—has found that her story of being fourteen and at camp fooling around with her troop leader's daughter is, she tells me, "actively distressing" to a certain type of person. "That's not the story you're supposed to tell," she continues. "My experience of telling that story has just been so illuminating to me about the ways in which that's the wrong story."

What is the right story? Shechter notes that there's a fetishization of the "perfect moment," when virginity loss involves someone you're deeply in love with, taking place in a romantic setting "with candles and your favorite band playing on the stereo." If you achieve this sort of ideal experience, the assumption seems to be that the rest of your romantic experiences will be similarly charmed; the converse, of course, being that "if you feel like you've done it wrong, it's like you've ruined your life."

On the subway, listening to my friends share the stories of their respective first times, I felt shame because—unlike them—my "first time" story wasn't sweet or cute or funny. The first man I attempted vaginal sex with didn't love me, or even particularly like me; he was a coworker who took me back to his mother's house in Bensonhurst after a night of drinking. What transpired that evening felt, on my end, like a lackluster, underwhelming, drunken sexual episode—but one that involved some degree of penile penetration, and thus virginity loss, nonetheless. But a few days later my coworker angrily informed me that, due to my apparently unaccommodating anatomy, nothing of the sort had transpired. The heterosexual virginity I'd been so desperate to shed was slapped back on me like a scarlet V; everything about the experience left me feeling damaged, inadequate, and unacceptable. When another hookup a few months later conclusively did away with any remaining remnants of my virginity, I didn't feel as though I'd gotten a second chance, or like this was my successful do over: that first, botched experience still felt definitive, a sign that—in the realm of heterosexual relationships—I was destined to be found flawed and wanting, and any experience that unfolded otherwise was merely the result of the extensive amount of effort I'd put in to transform myself from my natural, undesirable state.

This notion of one's first time as uniquely important is widespread in our culture. An article from a 2013 issue of *Journal of Sex & Marital Therapy* titled "Gone but Not Forgotten: Virginity Loss and Current Sexual Satisfaction" argues that "one's first-time sexual experience is more than just a milestone in development.... It appears to have implications for their sexual well-being years later."[8] Research scientists aren't the only ones pushing this line of thinking: virgins are widely assumed to imprint on their first sexual partner, emotionally attaching to that person and, presumably, judging all future sexual experiences by the yardstick of that inaugural encounter. Shechter describes this as a "universal idea that putting a penis into a vagina will change someone forever, that there is this one specific act that happens one time and it determines everything about you. Your morality, your desirability, the way you walk, the way you dress, everything is somehow determined."[9]

In the comics anthology *The Virgin Project*, artists K. D. Boze and Stasia Kato offer up a collection of virginity-loss stories, each one rendered as a quick comic tale. The anthology features a more diverse selection of tales than you might expect. The opening entry is an anonymous story of reportedly consensual incest, and the numerous tales from queer

[8] It should be noted that, like many psych studies, this one involved college students (331 of them, for the record), so, you know, all kinds of caveats apply.

[9] Even, oddly, if that first experience was your only experience, which Shechter notes gives someone the "imprimatur of not being a virgin anymore" for the rest of their (potentially sexless) life.

people offer a more complicated take on what "virginity" actually means. But even as it lightly takes the doctrine of virginity to task, *The Virgin Project* still manages to reify it. By virtue of its very existence, the book reinforces the importance of these first-time narratives, elevating the idea of first-time sex even as it offers up stories that question how important first times really are.[10]

Most of the experiences contained within the pages of *The Virgin Project* are positive and celebratory—unsurprising, given that people with fun, happy first-time stories are probably more likely to submit them to an anthology. But it's the handful of stories that push into darker territory that reveal the boundaries of how we're expected to lose our virginity. Five stories (four from women, one from a man) involve experiences of sexual assault; tellingly, the majority of these sexual assault survivors end their story by declaring that their sexual assault didn't "count" and wasn't their "real" first time.

It's not particularly surprising that assault survivors would prefer not to confer some magical, life-defining significance upon a horrific experience of trauma, but at the same time, there's something oddly telling about this reframing of what "loss of virginity" actually means. If first-time sex is purely defined by the physical act—if virginity loss is really just about that first penis in, or some other inaugural physical act—then redefining it shouldn't be possible. What these women seem to be getting at, though, is something else: it's less the physical aspect of loss of virginity that they're trying to redefine, and more the presumed transformative, life-defining magic

---

[10] Also, notably, none of the heterosexual narratives ever seem to question what "loss of virginity" actually means, all seemingly defaulting to the penis-in-vagina definition.

that they hope to reassign from an experience of trauma to one of consent.

Shechter tells me that, while doing research for her documentary, as well as curating an affiliated database of virginity-loss stories called The V-Card Diaries, she "heard from a lot of young women who had been sexually assaulted.... They feel like, 'This thing happened to me; this thing was taken from me; this thing has now established me as a certain thing. I will never get my virginity back; I have been changed against my will.'" There's an obvious experience of healing to be found in reclaiming the significance associated with virginity and assigning it a positive, affirming meaning. But the question still remains: Why do we need a significant "first time" at all?

"Virginity is a concept that is only as useful as you want it to be," Shechter continues. For some, it may be useful to treat one specific sexual experience as transformative, magical, and special—but if that idea causes pain, frustration, or trauma, why do we need to hold on to it?

Put another way: What is the societal benefit of the concept of virginity? Is there anything worth salvaging, or should we scrap it entirely, recognizing it as nothing more than an antiquated notion dreamt up by men for whom women's bodies were little more than offspring-producing property?

For all my hesitancy about the idea of virginity—particularly virginity that's constructed as a one-and-done, transformative experience that only involves the insertion of a penis into a vagina—I still have trouble letting go of it entirely. For all its fuzziness and lack of clarity, it still seems to be gesturing toward something vaguely worth considering, something that might explain why we have such trouble completely letting go of it.

For starters: there's no question that sexual intimacy introduces new pleasures, and new problems, into many people's lives. From a public health perspective, sexual activity increases the risk of being exposed to an STI or becoming pregnant, making it reasonable for a physician to want to know whether an STI screening is in order or if their patient might need an introduction to birth control.

But still, even here, virginity falls short. While the categories "virgin" and "nonvirgin" may gesture toward a collection of relevant information, they're far too broad to provide any actual clarity about a patient's risk factors or behaviors. A person who engaged in sex once twenty years ago may no longer be considered a virgin, but they're unlikely to be at risk for any sex-related maladies; on the flip side, a woman who's only engaged in anal sex may consider herself a "technical virgin," but that technicality alone won't reduce her risk of STI exposure.

In clinical settings, there's an increasing recognition of the limits to the labels society readily offers up to describe our sexual behavior.[11] Few doctors assess their patients' risk factors by asking about virginity; a more common way to approach the topic is by asking whether someone is sexually active. But even that question isn't super useful: as Blank—who teaches medical students how to do diagnostic interviewing effectively—tells me, there's a difference between knowing if someone's "sexually active" and knowing what kinds of sex they participate in with what gender of partners and what manner of safety precautions. To accurately assess a person's sexual health needs, we need far more insight

---

[11] Largely in response to the HIV/AIDS epidemic, which made getting specific, accurate information about sexual behavior that much more important.

than knowing whether they're a virgin—even knowing that someone considers themselves a virgin isn't enough to guarantee that they don't want, or need, access to STI screenings and contraceptives.

But even as virginity fails as a diagnostic tool, there's still an emotional and social importance to becoming someone whose sexuality involves the participation of other people. Eltahawy tells me that, as she began exploring her sexuality in her late twenties, "it was like dismantling this ivory tower of so-called virginity that I had been taught to build." Many of those experiences felt transgressive for her, each new experience helping to chip away at that tower. But it was still that traditional conception of virginity loss that felt the most important, most transgressive, to her. "When we actually did have PIV, it did feel like *the thing*," she tells me. "We'd been building up to it, and the fact that it had taken seven or eight months for me to feel ready for it is an indication that it was a big deal, that I was building up to it. I had waited so long. It did feel like a big deal."

Some of this is, doubtless, socially created. Becoming sexually intimate with other people feels significant because we're told it's significant; Eltahawy herself notes that her first experience with intercourse felt so deeply meaningful largely because of the social weight that society has placed on the act. Not everyone sees sexual intimacy as transformative, important, or even inherently desirable. There are asexual people who are perfectly content to live their entire lives without ever engaging in sexual intimacy; to assume they are somehow undeveloped or immature is to misunderstand the breadth of the human experience.

And even for those of us who do find meaning in sexual intimacy, this black-and-white, yes-or-no understanding of our identities is incredibly constricting. "As I grew older and I looked back on my adolescent experiences, I realized that [my first experience of intercourse] was a step in my sexual evolution that I had imbued with a lot of meaning," says Lena Chen, an artist and activist who organized the Rethinking Virginity conference as a student at Harvard. "But it was nonetheless just one pit stop on this bigger journey. And it was really hard to take the rest of the journey into account when you had one defining moment that you called virginity loss."

What if we could create a framework that preserves and honors that sense of wonder and excitement so many of us feel when experiencing intimacy for the first time while adding in a flexibility that allows us to decide for ourselves what matters and what "counts"? Shechter, for one, thinks we might benefit more from talking about "sexual milestones" rather than "virginity loss." One's first experience with vaginal intercourse can, of course, be an important sexual milestone—but so can first orgasm (with or without a partner), or first truly pleasurable sexual experience, or first sexual experience with someone we truly love, or first casual sex experience, or the first time we experience any of the countless sexual pleasures that there are to enjoy. "There's a lot of exploration that happens which we don't have a neatly defined category for," Chen tells me. Mutual masturbation, frottage, sex play involving vibrators and stimulation toys, pegging, and kink are all experiences that can radically alter our experiences of both our selves and our sexual identities. What would it look like if we honored those first times alongside our first experience of intercourse?

Or perhaps instead of putting so much weight on "first times," we allow ourselves to celebrate best times, or times that helped us understand ourselves better, or times when something really, truly clicked about how we experience sexual pleasure and what it really means to us. Sexuality is a rich, complex tapestry—the way we conceive and speak about our experiences should be allowed to reflect that reality.

Prior to the mid-twentieth century, "male virginity" wasn't really a concept; virgins, and virginity, were concepts exclusively applied to women.[12] To the extent that there was a male corollary to virginity, it was celibacy. Men who abstained from sex—regardless of whether they'd engaged in it at some point in their lives—were celibate. Celibacy could be taken up or abandoned at any point in time, completely unaffected by any past state, and unlike virginity, celibacy was not seen to wholly determine a man's worth.

With its focus on current behavior, rather than one particular point in time, celibacy is arguably the more useful label, making it odd that the concept has largely fallen out of favor, as virginity has been broadened to include people of all genders. But perhaps virginity continues to carry social weight because, unlike celibacy, it's an effective way of policing women's bodies and behavior.

Virginity, Blank tells me, is just one small segment of a larger narrative about "normal" sexuality. "But it's deeply connected with all of the other parts of that narrative," she continues. The way we talk about virginity is inextricable from the way we talk "about pleasure, about consent, about

---

[12] What gave rise to the male virgin? Shechter suspects that the writings of Philip Roth may have had something to do with it; Blank hypothesizes that the popularization of hormonal birth control—which removed one of the primary reasons for abstaining from sex—might have helped to degender the concept of "virgin."

desirability, about what kinds of sex you have or don't have, and what kinds of sex count and don't count." And the deeply uncomfortable truth is that a narrative that places emphasis on the notion of female virginity, one that roots that concept of virginity in a biological fiction, is a narrative that is deeply rigged against women.

Few American women are at risk of being subjected to the harshest consequences of purity culture: it is unlikely that state-sanctioned virginity tests or female genital mutilation will ever gain popularity within this country, and—despite the best efforts of the Religious Right—trends weigh heavily against a mass acceptance of abstaining from sex until marriage. But we're still guided by the very same principles that underpin those aggressive manifestations of misogyny. We still believe that virginity—or lack thereof—is one of the defining characteristics of a person; we still believe that it's made manifest in the female body and can be "proven" under the perfect set of circumstances. We still believe that virginity is real—and so long as we believe that, we've bought into a system where women can't win.

Yet women who dare to tell an uncomfortable truth, one that entirely upends the rules we've been told to follow, are rarely celebrated by society. More often, they're mocked, shamed, and shunned. "If you're lying to navigate a completely rigged system, that is just an act of self-preservation," Shechter tells me. Still, to call out the lie that is virginity is to set yourself up for retaliation and rebuke. It's a tremendous act of bravery that few have the stomach for.

But it's a kind of bravery Eltahawy is intimately familiar with. Over drinks, she pulls out her phone to show me an Egyptian newspaper that recently did a story on her. The Arabic text, she tells me, identifies her as a "sex activist"—"code for slut," she clarifies. Just below the headline, there's a photo of Eltahawy from a few years back, her arms in casts after being fractured while the police held her in custody. "They wanted to remind me, 'We did this to you, and we can do this to you again.'"

"Historically, the concept of virginity was a way to control and classify and possibly punish women," Shechter reminds me. In places like Egypt, women like Eltahawy deal regularly with that reality, actively resisting forces that attempt to reduce their entire worth as human beings to the status of their hymens. But even in America, our continued belief in something as imaginary as virginity—and our continued insistence that it's provable, that it's important, that it matters—suggests we may not have come as far as some of us would like to believe. As long as we hold on to the fairy tale of virginity, and its mythical accoutrements like the hymen, we'll be holding back women by continuing to teach them that there's a right way to exist as a sexual being—and we'll be giving them incentives to dissemble and deceive, as a way to fit in, as a way to fade into the background, as a way, quite frankly, to survive.

In the Middle East, Eltahawy tells me, many cultures "use the word 'girl' for an unmarried person who is female at birth, until she is made a woman through a penis." This notion of becoming a woman through intercourse and sexual activity is not unique to Arab cultures, of course—American pop culture is rife with mentions of the phenomenon—but it is worth noting that, however much importance we may place on deflowering, sex is not the only way one becomes a woman.

In adolescence, most of us go through puberty; biologically, if not socially, this is the process by which girls are transformed into women. Yet paradoxically, some of the secondary sexual characteristics intimately tied to female puberty—the body hair, the acne, the inevitable weight gain—are treated as affronts to a woman's femininity. To be a woman in this world, it's not enough to merely exist in a body that's been designated female. If you want to be taken seriously, you truly have to work for it, buffing and polishing and reshaping your body until it conforms to the ideals set forth by our culture. Succeeding as a woman requires living up to a punishing standard: clear skin, a beautiful face, a gym-toned body, gravity-defying breasts, and perfectly coiffed hair,[13] all of which you're expected to achieve without any visible effort.

It's a requirement that's so pervasive, and so accepted, that there's an entire industry built on it—and, perhaps unsurprisingly, it's a requirement that opens up yet another opportunity for women to be accused of deceit.

---

[13] On your head, that is—everywhere else is an entirely different story.

❚ CHAPTER FOUR ❚

I Woke Up Like This

A WHILE BACK, Baze Mpinja decided to stop relaxing her hair and go natural again. At first she straightened her natural hair so that it would blend into the relaxed hair as she grew it out, but eventually—tired of dealing with two different textures of hair—she decided to get a weave to help her get through the last stages of growing out.

The weave, Mpinja tells me over coffee, was long, straight, thick, and dark. And going out into the world with that hair, rather than the relaxed hair she'd had for years, or the afro she has now, made for a wildly different experience. "The reaction that I got with that hair was dramatically different," she says. Specifically, the hair got her attention from men—in particular, from nonblack men who rarely looked her way on other days. "I definitely saw a noticeable difference in the number of white men that would look at me," she shares.

For Mpinja—a longtime beauty editor who's worked at publications like *Suede*, *Vibe Vixen*, *Glamour*, and *xoJane*—the weave was just a temporary look, not an essential aspect of her identity or the only way that she could feel pretty. But the surge of attention it generated gave her a glimpse into a whole other way of life, and a new perspective on the appeal of enhanced hair. To be able to step into a world where all eyes were on her, merely through the addition of some

luscious, long locks? "I definitely see how it's hard to give
that up. It's hard to give that validation up," she says, and
had she been someone else, she might have been convinced
to permanently commit to a weave. But she didn't consider
the experience a positive one. "Instead of getting an ego
boost, it made me sad, like, 'Gosh, I didn't realize how invisible I was without it.' That was the biggest takeaway: I'm
fucking invisible without this hair.'"

I've never had a weave or extensions, but the story Mpinja
told me was nevertheless familiar. The idea that there's a
magic accessory out there—be it fake hair, shapewear, or just
the right shade of eye shadow—that can dramatically transform our lives and launch us on the course to happiness is a
common one among women. Whole sections of the beauty
and fashion industries hawk their products as the key to a
successful life, and countless rom coms have been pitched
on the premise that if a woman merely takes off her glasses
and lets her hair down, she'll be able to find true love. Indeed, this premise was so prevalent during my adolescence
that it was something of a shock to discover, at the age of
twelve, that swapping glasses for contacts didn't immediately
land me a boyfriend.

And while the idea that lasting, eternal happiness is just
one cosmetic purchase away may be a bit overblown, there's
no question that there are tangible rewards to be had by anyone who masters the art of beauty. The attention Mpinja
received for her weave is just the tip of the iceberg: studies
have shown that women who wear makeup at work make
more money, literally cashing in on the perks provided to
attractive people. Wearing makeup can boost a woman's confidence and self-assuredness. It can also make other people
see her as not just prettier but healthier, more competent,

and higher status: a 2006 study published in the *Journal of Applied Social Psychology* reported that "makeup has a beneficial impact upon the perception of a woman's earning potential, professional class, health, and confidence." And for women of color, these beauty tricks can be a way to adapt to, and survive in, a world that all too often equates "beautiful" with "white."

Yet for all the benefits secured by women who deftly wield a makeup brush or wig or shapewear, there's a danger that comes with being too good at transforming one's self into the ideal image of female beauty. In January 2015, makeup artist Andreigha Wazny posted two photos of her friend Ashley VanPevenage, one showing VanPevenage without makeup, the next showing her with a fully made-up, high-glamour face. The transformation is stark: VanPevenage's skin goes from blemished to flawless, her nose appears to change shape, her eyebrows darken and fill out, and her eyes—now framed by dark, smoky eye shadow and lustrous black lashes—seem brighter and more radiant. To anyone familiar with the transformative power of makeup, there was nothing particularly surprising about these before and after shots. But when they went viral, launching out of the orbit of makeup social media and into the mainstream internet, things took a dark turn.

A few weeks after Wazny posted the photos, a Twitter user reposted them with the caption "The reason why you gotta take a bitch swimming on the first date,"[1] an outing that would presumably wash away a woman's makeup and reveal her "true" face. The implication of the phrase, which

---

[1] A phrase, it should be noted, that did not originate with this user, but seemed to explode in popularity subsequent to this exchange.

eventually turned into a meme itself, was clear. Women are trying to deceive men, using the various tricks of the beauty industry to lure unsuspecting paramours into relationships. A man who isn't careful—who takes the object of his affection at face value, so to speak—can easily wind up saddled to a woman who's merely faking the attractive exterior that drew him to her in the first place. Women, it's implied, are inherently deceitful, and those who manage to secure through makeup what they were denied by nature deserve to be revealed.

For women, the world of beauty often presents a difficult, if not outright impossible, situation to navigate. Eschew cosmetics entirely, and you'll likely be scorned for not caring enough about your appearance; put too much faith in the power of physical transformation, and suddenly you're a grotesque caricature of vanity as well as a portrait of deceit. There is, in theory, an optimal amount of effort that deftly balances looking attractive with not caring too much about your appearance, but where that perfect mix is can be pretty hard to pinpoint—and where, exactly, it lies depends a lot on what sort of looks you were born with.

"Take a bitch swimming on the first date" may be one of the more vicious male commentaries on female makeup use, but it's hardly the only one. Men have long declared themselves the arbiters of acceptable application of makeup, and the internet is filled with anti-makeup screeds that use photos to illustrate the argument that women who are unadorned and au naturel look far better than "cakefaces" who bury their skin under layers of product.

Why the animosity toward makeup? Some of it is undoubtedly due to a suspicion that women who wear makeup are trying to hide something (presumably a hideous appearance), but there's also a vague sense that women who eschew cosmetics are of an entirely different—and more desirable—breed than their bedecked peers. A *Men's Health* piece offering itself up as "an ode to natural beauty" presents a collection of reasons why bare faces are better; for readers of *Men's Health* it's clear that makeup isn't just makeup. According to the experts cited in the piece, going makeup-free makes women seem more confident, more innocent, and more "primal" and sexy,[2] as well as suggesting that they're outdoorsy, approachable, and down-to-earth. The general sentiment—which pervades virtually all arguments against makeup—seems to be that women who eschew beauty culture are more authentic and, as a result, inherently better partners.

Which, I suppose, makes it that much more ironic that the photos chosen to illustrate this celebration of going makeup-free are all stock images secured from Thinkstock—photos that, unsurprisingly, are definitely showcasing women who are wearing makeup. This isn't just a mistake on the part of *Men's Health*; it's a common trait of articles claiming to celebrate going makeup-free. If anything, men who try to use photos to "prove" they hate makeup are more likely to offer up a demonstration of how little they know about how makeup works and what role it plays in many women's daily routines. The "makeup-free" women celebrated by men are rarely truly makeup-free; rather, they're either wearing sparse amounts of carefully applied product or

---

[2] How a lack of makeup simultaneously makes women seem less sexually experienced and more "primal" is a mystery to me.

employing the oxymoronic cosmetic strategy known as "natural makeup."

For those not steeped in the lingo of fashion magazines, practitioners of the natural makeup look use cosmetics to create a visage perhaps best described as "you, but better." There's a great deal of emphasis placed on making the skin look flawless; blush, subtle eye shadow, muted lipstick, and mascara all come into play to help make facial features pop and add depth and definition to features that might not stand out without cosmetic assistance. It's a look that's supposed to suggest effortless beauty, but as anyone who's actually put it into practice can tell you, it often takes more effort than a heavier, obviously made-up look.

Devoting the better part of an hour to making yourself look as if you're not wearing makeup at all may seem like a counterproductive task, but for women with acne scars or eye bags or unwanted facial hair, it can be a way to feel pretty without looking overly made-up. When I ask Mpinja for her thoughts on the look, she offers another possibility for its popularity. Natural makeup, she tells me, allows women to conform to conventional beauty standards without advertising the fact that they're trying. "You're supposed to hide the work that goes into looking pretty," Mpinja notes. "If you admit how much effort you're putting in, it begs the question why"; specifically it suggests that you're vain or desperate for male attention, undesirable qualities even within a society that teaches women to measure their worth by the amount of attention men give them for their appearances.

But let's be clear about something: looking pretty, by American beauty standards, takes a lot of effort—no matter how genetically gifted you may be. Even if you're blessed with clear skin and an even complexion; thick, healthy hair;

long, dark eyelashes; a stunning bone structure; and enviably pouty lips, to be considered truly beautiful requires adherence to all manner of painful, time-consuming rituals designed to remake the female body into an artificially soft, smooth, and hairless "ideal." And if you're not white, it's that much harder: the faces and features most readily celebrated in our culture all hew to a Eurocentric beauty standard.

What kind of work goes into being pretty? The first episode of the CW's *Crazy Ex-Girlfriend* offers a glimpse into some of the complicated, and at times grotesque, practices that have been normalized by American beauty culture. As Rachel Bloom performs "The Sexy Getting Ready Song," an R & B tribute to the work women put into physically prepping themselves for a romantic encounter, a variety of ablutions are depicted on-screen. Among those that make an appearance are eyebrow plucking, nose hair plucking, heel buffing, donning Spanx, exfoliating facial skin, curling eyelashes, curling hair, bleaching facial hair, and—in a scene that ends with a shot of blood spattered on the bathroom wall—self-administered waxing of the hair inside her buttocks. Though the beauty rituals are played for comic effect, they're very much rooted in reality; indeed, some women's cosmetic routines are far more punishing than what makes it into the song.

So much about the ideal women are taught to aspire to—the gravity-defying yet ample breasts, the silky smooth skin, the muscular yet buxom body—is an artificial construct, effortlessly available to only a tiny minority of women (if to any of us at all); for the rest of us, achieving the look takes a staggering amount of work. Any woman who's tried to be pretty knows exactly how much time, effort, and pain are required to adhere to beauty standards. Yet even as we all know what goes on behind the scenes, we're still playing a perverse little game that asks us to obscure the work, to publicly be in denial about the effort it takes to be an attractive woman.[3] It's not enough to convincingly present a flawlessly attractive exterior; we must do all that while professing to the world that it was all effortless, that—to paraphrase Beyoncé—we simply woke up this way.

But to deny the labor that goes into female beauty is to prop up the lie that it's "natural" to have a body that is anything but, that the aggressive beauty standards we're judged by are not just acceptable but potentially even fair. When body hair is treated as an invading army to be battled and defeated rather than a simple secondary sex characteristic, the phrase "natural beauty" ceases to have meaning. We've bought into the notion that it's not merely desirable but downright mandatory to invest time and money and effort into maintaining this charade of what "real women" look like—even as that charade reinforces some of the most noxious aspects of American society.

"Looking black used to be almost illegal." That's one of the first things that Tia Williams, a beauty editor turned copy director at hair care company Bumble and bumble, tells me as we sit in the café area of the Bumble and bumble salon. "The more you met that Western [beauty ideal], the easier it was for you to get a job, the easier it was for you to exist in America."

---

[3] And, to some degree, to obscure the work it takes to be a woman, period. An essay penned by Jessica Leigh Hester for the *Atlantic* argues that concealer, foundation, and other makeup tricks used to make women look less tired are, in effect, preventing the rest of the world from seeing how tiring it is to live in this world as a woman.

For Williams, this context is essential for any discussion about black women and beauty culture and, in particular, black women and hair. Though black women who choose to alter or enhance their appearance through artificial means—for instance, the weave, fake eyes, and fake nails alternately celebrated and mocked by Outkast in "We Luv Deez Hoez"—are often assumed to be coming from some shallow, superficial place, "it's deeply rooted in trying to assimilate, in trying to go out into the workforce and make money to feed your babies. It isn't just a beauty statement. It comes from a place of survival."

While American ideas about beauty have expanded over the years, the legacy of treating white features as inherently superior still casts a long shadow over what we consider attractive. Black women—indeed, all women, of all races and ethnicities—are still held to a beauty standard that privileges the features of a certain kind of white woman over everyone else, a beauty standard that plays out on the runway, in fashion magazines, in advertising, and on film.

"The racial beauty hierarchy that exists in America is so internalized," Williams tells me, that most of the people who reinforce it don't even see what they're doing. Williams doesn't believe that the powers that be in the fashion and entertainment industries are intentionally communicating that white is beautiful and black is ugly, but—having grown up in a culture that bombards us with the idea that white is normal—we're too often oblivious to the ways we erase diversity and normalize whiteness as the default beauty standard.

It's a hierarchy that puts black women in America in an unenviable position, one Williams is all too familiar with. "You grow up thinking that a lighter-skinned woman is more beautiful, a black girl with straighter hair is more desirable, a certain body type is more desirable, and you set up black women to meet all these standards, and when they break their back to do so, you vilify them and demonize them." If you're naturally far from the ideal, you're made to feel that you're worthless; if you achieve the ideal through fakery, you run the risk of being mocked for being a cheat. To be a specific kind of beautiful is all important, but to go out of your way to achieve beauty makes you shallow, selfish, and vain.

It's true that we are chipping away at the narrow standards of female beauty that have encouraged so many women to aspire to—for want of a better term—"look white." A world where a dark-skinned, natural-haired woman like Lupita Nyong'o is featured on mainstream magazine covers is certainly one that's begun to open up its ideas of who gets to be considered pretty. But it's worth noting that even as women like Nyong'o are embraced by publications and advertising geared toward the female gaze, male-oriented publications and ads are still celebrating a more limited definition of beauty, one that presents light skin and long straight hair as the apexes of female beauty. During its eleven-year run, *King Magazine*—a popular lifestyle magazine aimed at black men—featured more nonblack women than women with afros on its covers, with a clear preference toward women with long, flowing locks and lighter skin. Natural hair and dark skin still aren't really being marketed to men as sexy—and if you're a woman who's interested in attracting the attention of men, that kind of messaging matters.

In a society that privileges white beauty above all others, women of color have added incentive to alter their

appearances in order to fit in, find love, and get by. But artificially created—or at least enhanced—beauty knows no
racial bounds, and indeed, these days, the famous women
most readily associated with fakery are white.

"The Kardashians tricked everyone," Williams tells me,
thinking back to the late aughts, when the sisters emerged
on the scene. "They had tons of weave in their hair." Though
artificially enhanced hair was hardly a new beauty tactic, the
sisters hid their work so well that even a beauty editor like
Williams was baffled by how the women achieved such vo-
luminous locks. "I remember asking my girlfriend, 'Is it because they're Armenian?'"

Fake hair was just the beginning of the Kardashian sisters'
embrace of artificial enhancement. Over the past decade,
the family—and in particular, the omnipresent Kim—has
been associated with all manner of beauty tricks. Heavy
makeup, lash extensions, lip injections, and all manner of
cosmetic surgeries: if you can think of a beauty procedure,
someone's associated it with some member of the Kardashian clan, and whether it's a rumor doesn't even really
matter. The Kardashians have never hidden their penchant
for artifice; to some degree, it's even part of their appeal.

Kylie Jenner, the youngest member of the Kardashian
clan, was ten years old when the TV show *Keeping Up with
the Kardashians* debuted. She's literally grown up in public,
with scores of publications documenting her transition from
prepubescent child to glamorous young adult, keeping a run-
ning commentary on all the products and procedures she's
used along the way. Unlike other starlets, who might demur
about cosmetic surgery with talk of "deviated septums" and
other euphemisms, Jenner speaks openly about her use of
lip fillers, telling the *New York Times*, "I go to Dr. Ourian in

Beverly Hills. He's the best, and he's super natural about it. ... I would recommend that anyone who gets it done go for a filler that lasts only two to four months. It's annoying to keep going back, but you have the option of stopping it." There's something aspirational about the degree to which the Kardashians' beauty is artificial: the knowledge that so much of it was bought, rather than born with, suggests that any of us, anywhere, might one day achieve what these women have (provided, of course, that we're willing and able to spend the time, money, and effort on getting the look).

But that obvious artifice also seems to be part of why they inspire such rage. The most common criticism of the Kardashians is that they are somehow undeserving of their fame and fortune; they don't bring any real talent to the table aside from their looks, and even that isn't genuine. If they'd been born with their beauty, perhaps their ascension would somehow be "fair," but to fake one's way into that kind of fame is, apparently, crass and unseemly.

How despised are the Kardashians? So much so that *Cosmopolitan* once compiled a twenty-four-point list solely made up of celebrities dissing the family.[4] Even suffering a major trauma wasn't enough to garner Kim Kardashian sympathy: just days after she was robbed at gunpoint, the *Telegraph* ran a biting op-ed that opened with the author declaring her hatred of the reality star, then going on to make digs about her presumably fake face and body.

Yet even despite the intense, often nonstop backlash against their artifice, the Kardashians continue to reap extensive rewards. Their long-running reality show racks up awards and

---

[4] Among the more baffling entries on the list? Former models Janice Dickinson and Fabio, who, one could argue, didn't do that much more to earn their fame and fortune than the Kardashians.

churns out spin-offs, spawning popular apps and a mind-bogglingly successful business empire. Kim, on her end, shrugs off the "no talent" digs by pointing to her net worth as de facto evidence of her capability. When asked about her talents during a *60 Minutes* segment, Kim tells interviewer Bill Whitaker, "It is a talent to have a brand that's really successful." Even if that success is a product of something as intangible as her likability (or, others might argue, her shamelessness), Kim notes, its refusal to flame out seems to indicate that it "has to involve some kind of talent." Whatever mockery the family may endure, the fame, fortune, and access to America's elite institutions serve as undeniable proof that they're doing something right.

However much we may be taught to despise and disdain fakery, we nevertheless celebrate women who manage to fit our punishing, limited criteria for beauty—and, in many cases, strive to emulate them. In the summer of 2017, Kim launched her very own line of contouring kits under the name KKW Beauty, explicitly connecting her brand to an extreme makeup technique she's been both derided and celebrated for relying on. Some of the shades sold out within mere minutes of KKW Beauty's launch.

The benefits of being beautiful far outstrip any punishment for being inauthentic: the Kardashians, truly, are living proof.

In theory, I suppose, the men who rail against the "trickery" of makeup would prefer that the women of the world embrace honesty by existing in the world barefaced at all times—and oddly, this puts them in agreement with a certain breed of feminist.

There have always been women who've advocated against cosmetics; indeed, rejection of makeup was a hallmark of many a second-wave feminist. But in 2016, the anti-makeup sentiment popped up somewhere surprising: Hollywood. Celebrities including Alicia Keys, who took to the Lena Dunham–backed newsletter *Lenny Letter* to opine about her experiences eschewing cosmetics, and Mila Kunis, who appeared sans makeup on the cover of *Glamour*'s August 2016 issue, were the most prominent examples of what came to be known as the #nomakeup movement; all over social media, young women shared selfies showcasing their own cosmetic-free faces.

This celebration of going makeup-free is more than just an acknowledgment that makeup isn't for everyone; like many celebrity-endorsed trends, the movement has an almost religious fervor. In her *Lenny Letter* essay, Keys notes that, without makeup, she became "the strongest, most empowered, most free, and most honestly beautiful that I have ever felt," as though by rejecting a collection of powders and serums she'd somehow achieved enlightenment.

Framing the rejection of cosmetics as a moral stance rather than a personal choice is not unique to the no-makeup movement. Williams tells me that a similar attitude can be found in certain corners of the natural hair movement, where abandoning relaxer and fake hair is positioned not merely as a preference but as a sign of moral superiority. And yet as much as these movements claim to be about self-love and embracing authenticity, they still position physical beauty as the measure of a woman's worth. Keys doesn't talk about abandoning heavy makeup because she realized there are other things more important than her appearance. Her no-makeup stance pivots on the realization that even without makeup, she's still conventionally attractive—a claim that, quite frankly, many women cannot make.

Scrolling through the #nomakeup page on Instagram, one mostly finds pictures of women eager to demonstrate their "bravery" by allowing the world to see what their enviable bone structure and clear skin look like when they're not obscured by makeup. It's rare to see, say, women with blemished skin or dark circles under their eyes or even pale, thin eyelashes[5] posting their makeup-free faces—perhaps because most women are aware that you only get celebrated for going makeup-free when you're able to present a face that might as well be wearing makeup.

Williams pulls no punches when I ask for her take on the no-makeup trend. "I think it's antiwoman," she says. Though encouraging women to embrace their unmodified appearance has the potential to be a radical movement to encourage self-love and personal choice, that's not the result we've ended up with. No one gets celebrated for going makeup-free with cystic acne or hyperpigmentation; on the contrary, "you'll see being celebrated for not wearing makeup but having perfectly toned, even skin, naturally rosy cheeks, and a dewy luster"—and pretty much that alone. However strong, empowered, free, and beautiful Keys may have felt without her makeup on,[6] it's harder to imagine feeling that way if your no-makeup look leads strangers to ask if you're sick or tired—or to outright ignore you or treat you with disdain.

---

[5] In a somewhat perverse cooptation of the hashtag, I did see a number of ads for eyelash extensions promoted as #nomakeup.

[6] And it remains unclear just how makeup-free Keys actually went: *Cosmopolitan* later reported that, in addition to skin care treatments involving a jade roller, Keys's "no makeup" routine involved the use of Anastasia brow pencil, Vita Liberata's glowy serum, and Mally magical antishine mattifier.

As long as women are judged by their looks first, and as long as those looks are expected to hew to a punishingly narrow standard, most of us don't have the option to just "be ourselves." For all the problems that makeup creates, it at least offers the opportunity to level the playing field somewhat, taking appearance out of the equation and allowing our other qualities to shine through.

And even beyond the practical benefits of wearing makeup, there's also the question of why anyone else needs to care about what a woman deems necessary, beautiful, or just fun to do with her own face. "If you feel most comfortable in drag, be in drag," Williams declares—and it's hard for me to find a real reason to disagree with that.

"I understand why women wear makeup; I understand why women do their hair; I understand why women wear shapewear," Harnaam Kaur tells me. "People embrace and love what's fake."

Kaur, a London-based activist who champions body positivity and fights against bullying, is a member of the 10 percent of women who live with polycystic ovary syndrome (PCOS), a hormonal imbalance that can result in irregular menstrual cycles, acne, weight gain, skin tags, and hirsutism. In Kaur's case, PCOS has resulted in a thick, lush beard—one that, she tells me, is much fuller and thicker than that of many men.

Kaur is frequently treated as an outlier, the mythical bearded woman whose body pushes the boundaries of the gender binary. She's regularly celebrated as a fierce, feminist voice, appearing on lists as an inspirational model of nonconventional beauty and a radical example of self-acceptance. Yet to the extent that Kaur is unique, it's largely by a matter of degree. Female beards may be a relative rarity, but women with some amount of facial hair are hardly uncommon. According to some estimates, upwards of 40 percent of women have some sort of facial hair, the degree of hairiness often determined by the woman's race.[7]

If female facial hair is all around us, why are we so insistent that women are "naturally" hairless? Here, Kaur's experiences as a prominent hairy woman offer some insight: "I've had women approach me saying, 'I've been married with my partner for so and so years, and he still doesn't know that I get up every day to shave my face,'" she tells me. It's waxing, tweezing, bleaching, and threading—often conducted in secret—that render many a female face smooth, not some inborn female tendency toward completely bare faces.

It's not hard to see why women are so dedicated to eradicating their facial hair. We get told, over and over, that facial hair is a male attribute, that women who sport it are ugly, ill, or obscene. A 2013 poll conducted by Oxygen Media cited female facial hair as the number one turnoff for men;[8] while queer women can be more forgiving, mustaches are still most frequently sported by those who identify as butch. Even in medical and scientific contexts, a woman's mustache is never just a mustache. It's "unwanted"; it's "excessive"; it's not merely hairiness but "hirsutism," a term that sounds more indicative of monstrousness than natural variation. And women who choose to embrace their hairiness often have a hard time out in the world, even when they're

---

[7] One study found that Indian and Italian women are among the most likely to sport mustaches, a finding that will come as no surprise to anyone who's patronized a boutique that specializes in waxing or threading.

[8] Women, in contrast, rejected men for bad body odor.

as confident and self-assured as Kaur. "I still struggle with anxiety going out in public," Kaur tells me, noting that a decade of being bullied has provided her with a deeply upsetting awareness of what happens when bearded women dare to leave their homes.

Facial hair isn't the only element of women's natural bodies that's been cast as "unnatural" and unfeminine. There's a limit to what forms of "natural" beauty we celebrate; our communal conception of a woman's body is one born of artifice. Masculinity is, by and large, presented as the male body in an unmodified state. To grow body hair, to leave one's body untended, even to smell bad: all of that exists within the realm of normal, acceptable masculine presentation. Femininity, on the other hand, is inextricably connected to processes of remaking and reshaping the body in pursuit of some kind of artificial ideal. All femininity is, to some degree, a kind of drag; we're just more likely to call it out when the person performing it was assigned male at birth.

"This entire emphasis on the natural is really fascinating, and very weird given the tension between the natural and the artificial for trans women," writer Meredith Talusan tells me as we sit at her dining room table.

Mainstream, cisgender discussions of trans women tend to present the gender confirmation process as a collection of expensive surgeries: public commentary on Caitlyn Jenner's transition has included wide-eyed estimates of how much the athlete turned reality star must have spent in pursuit of her new face and form. Tabloids have detailed an array of rarely discussed surgeries presumed to have been purchased by Jenner, tossing around phrases like "brow bossing," "tracheal shaving," and "cheek implants" in an attempt to explain how she went from ultramasculine decathlete to the high femme *Vanity Fair* cover girl.

There is no question that some trans women pursue facial feminization, breast implants, and other expensive surgeries in an attempt to create an exterior that feels comfortable, just as there's no question that many cis women get all kinds of cosmetic surgery—in some cases, the exact same procedures pursued by trans women—in order to feel more beautiful, more feminine, happier with their own bodies.

But the notion that all trans women's faces and bodies are a product of surgical artifice is as misguided as our conviction that there's some "natural" and unified way to be a woman. Talusan, on her part, is a "natural" woman insomuch as the face she presents to the world is one unmodified by surgical intervention, but she readily acknowledges that her ability to move easily through the world as a trans woman who largely eschews makeup, her ability to be read by the world as a woman, and an attractive one at that, is largely due to luck of the draw and a random convergence of a handful of genetic and social factors.

Talusan is Filipina, but she's also albino, a rare combination that lends her the appearance of a petite white woman rather than one who's broad-shouldered and somewhat tall as far as Asian woman go. "I somehow, in this specific American context, ended up in this position of being a part of that group that is idealized as cisnormatively beautiful. Except for the fact that I'm trans."

Talusan has seen firsthand just how much easier life can be when you're perceived as a beautiful woman rather than an ugly, or even average, one. Even her transition process was aided by her appearance. At the time of her transition, it was standard procedure for trans women to be in therapy for six months before being granted access to hormones and then another year or so until gender confirmation surgery would be approved. Talusan, on the other hand, was given hormones at her first doctor's appointment—and told that she could be approved for surgery as soon as she desired it. "If you look at all of my medical documents, one of the things that it always says is, 'You wouldn't be able to tell she's trans and that makes her a really good candidate for medical transition,'" she tells me. "What would have cost other people other time and money, I didn't have to go through because of the fact that I could present myself credibly as a cis-passing woman immediately," without any of the extensive surgeries presumed to be de rigueur among trans women.

There was another privilege that Talusan experienced in transition. Right as she was beginning to publicly present as a woman, she also happened to be doing research into facial attractiveness—a project that brought with it a $10,000 budget for makeup. Talusan used this fund to embark on what she refers to as The Woman Project, learning to apply makeup and pluck her eyebrows and perform all the ablutions associated with female beauty. The benefits of adhering to widely accepted beauty standards quickly became apparent. When Talusan exemplified the ideal of a young, thin, femme woman, she received perks like discounts at independent boutiques and sometimes even free clothes. "People give you stuff if they think you look like a model," she tells me. "That's just a thing that happens."

As Talusan became more secure in her identity, she stopped wearing makeup. And when she did, those discounts dried up. Decreased access to luxury goods didn't particularly trouble her. Makeup had always been more a way to ensure that she'd be correctly gendered than an effort to conform to some abstract ideal of beauty, and once she knew that she'd be read as a woman with or without makeup, spending every day applying a kind of facial uniform began to seem woefully inefficient and unappealing.

But she still found herself surprised by the widespread expectations of how she, as a woman in her twenties, should be performing beauty and applying makeup and adhering to these norms and standards of appearance. Whether or not makeup felt personally important or necessary, there was an assumption that as a professional young woman who wanted to be hip, who wanted to be cool, she would ultimately comply. There was an assumption that, as a woman, a made-up exterior was something she owed to others—to her friends, to her employer, to the world—and that assumption was one she found fundamentally baffling.

"We live in an artificial world," Talusan notes. There is virtually nothing "natural" about our concepts of female beauty, nor are our standards for how women are to comport themselves in any way based in some sort of prehistoric state of nature. Being perceived as beautiful primarily means being born in the right place, at the right time, with the type of features and body that happen to be currently celebrated, as well as being willing to put in the work to adhere to whatever unnatural beauty standards are currently considered desirable. And yet—even knowing all this, even knowing how random and unfair and nonsensical beauty often is—we still present "natural" beauty as not merely a real thing, but even an admirable, notable achievement.

"It's hard to imagine how much makeup someone I know would have to wear to look like a completely different person," Mpinja tells me. "Even if you had on a lot of makeup right now, and then I saw you the next day, I don't think I'd be like, 'Hey, where is she? I don't recognize her!' It's such a dramatic concept to say that a woman is unrecognizable without makeup."

Mpinja ticks off some of the makeup tricks that might obscure someone's actual appearance—"a Kardashian level of foundation and contouring" or fake lashes, perhaps—but even then, she tells me, "you can see that the person is wearing it. Did you think they always wear it? They have to take it off at some point."

That reality—that the makeup has to come off eventually, that the shapewear must go back in the drawer, that hair grows out, and acrylic nails don't last forever—is one that only seems to come as a surprise to men. Women know they're playing a rigged game, but they play it the best that they can because they have no other choice. It's only men who, like Nick Dunne in *Gone Girl*, seem stunned to discover that the Cool Girl they've taken home with them is a real, human woman underneath.

"We expect that at some point we can relax," Mpinja tells me, commenting that, among other things, women "know that our legs aren't always perfectly shaved." And yet all the pressure to be perfect, to live up to a standard, can create "some anxiety about the reveal," fueling a fear that the moment we let our guard down might be the moment we get rejected. To get to the point where we can show our real faces, our real bodies, our real hair is to achieve a level of true intimacy—but the path to that point is a fraught and difficult one to traverse.

There's a scene in the movie *Bridget Jones's Diary* that encapsulates the anxiety many women deal with every day.

Preparing for an evening out, Jones surveys two different pairs of underwear: the unsightly, enormous Spanx[9] that will mold her body into a form she considers more appealing, and the barely there panties that encapsulate the air of sexy fun she'd like to communicate to anyone who ends up seeing her in her underwear. We're supposed to be the fun, sexy girl with the flawless body—but we're not supposed to show the work that it takes to get that body, or that face, or that hair, to begin with. You have to be beautiful if you want to win the game, but beauty requires effort, and visible effort can get you disqualified. It often feels as if there's no way to win—unless, perhaps, you're a part of an industry that profits off of promises to help women game the system.

Beauty culture is pervasive, infiltrating every space that women exist in—even ones where appearances aren't supposed to matter. Despite its origins as a text-driven medium, the internet has evolved into a visual space. Selfies are as essential to the ecosystem as 280-character sound bites and cute cat videos, creating, as Jenna Wortham once wrote, "a kind of visual diary, a way to mark our short existence and hold it up to others as proof that we were here." Yet while the opportunity to inject our own faces into our digital missives has given social media a more intimate, personal feel, it's also upped the pressure to make sure that we're putting our best face forward.

As selfies have become de rigueur, they've given rise to an industry devoted to digital beauty tools and an explosion of cheap (or free) photo editing apps that make it easier than

---

[9] Allegedly this scene caused a spike in the sales of Spanx, for reasons that I will never understand.

ever to get a digital facelift. With the click of a button, you can put your best selfie forward, no matter what your actual face looks like, using standalone makeover apps like Meitu and YouCam or filter packs built into popular photo sharing apps like Snapchat and Instagram.

In theory, these photo filters are gender neutral, able to be used by anyone. In practice, it's clear that they're intended primarily for women and girls,[10] offering up a one-click way to look cuter, younger, and more feminine. According to Amanda Hess, a *New York Times* writer who profiled photo filters in an episode of her web series, Internetting with Amanda Hess, the aesthetic favored by many photo filter platforms is "extremely girlish." "Everything becomes more diminutive," says Hess, noting that even filters that offer users an opportunity to engage in more radical transformations still enforce this cute, feminine aesthetic. "If I want to turn myself into a bear...I can't turn myself into a scary bear. It has to be a bear that makes my face look like a tiny anime face with huge eyes, and then I have sparkly bear ears." Even in the most outrageous fantasy filters, "the beauty ideals are baked in."[11] For all their newfangled features, these filters are, in many ways, a more limited form of beauty enhancement, one that constrains the user's options and speaks volumes about beauty standards in the process. There may be "right" and "wrong" ways to go about applying

---

[10] Why are filters so gendered? Hess suspects it's related to the fact that women are taught to present themselves as objects to be consumed in a way that men just aren't. "I've never really heard anything about the visual presence of men on Snapchat," she muses, noting that men's online personas are more often about creating content rather than merely being seen.

[11] Also in the theoretically more grounded filters. In March 2017, Snapchat faced blowback after debuting a Marie Curie–themed filter for International Women's Day that digitally applied eye makeup and fake eyelashes to users.

makeup, but there's still a playfulness and creativity granted to the wearer. Filters, in contrast, offer no such freedom. Either you use them or you don't. And if you do, you're locked into a very specific vision of what "beauty" looks like: one that privileges a glittery, anime-style femininity to the exclusion of all others.

Filters are, in effect, a heightened version of enhancement in real life. The beauty standards peddled are more specific (and more unrealistic); the vague and often intangible benefits of being pretty are rendered concrete[12] in the form of likes, views, and additional followers. The resulting dynamic echoes what we see with real-world beauty. In our popularity-obsessed culture, women who don't employ filters are at a competitive disadvantage, working to secure likes without using all the tools and options available to them. And, just like makeup, filters have also sparked their own "authenticity"-driven backlash. There's a #nofilter movement that parallels the "natural" beauty advocacy of #nomakeup—women who are deemed to rely too heavily on photo filters are just as likely to be scorned as those outed for their "excessive" use of makeup.

Yet for all the ways that photo filters replicate and enhance the dynamics of makeup and other real-world beauty tricks, what I find particularly intriguing is an oft-overlooked benefit that Hess explains to me. For Hess, filters aren't about improving her appearance, conforming to beauty standards, or increasing her "like" count. They're about safety.

"It can feel a lot more comfortable to be like, 'This is Snapchat me, with modifications of my face provided by Snapchat,'" Hess tells me. "That's not me trying to trick anybody,

---

[12] Or as concrete as digital commentary can be, anyway.

it's more like me feeling comfortable engaging [online] without feeling like I'm putting my whole self out there." Social media culture, she tells me, asks participants to constantly put their image out into the world. For women, that can be "a super fraught ask," she says, one that opens them up to snide commentary, personal attacks, and trolling. "The filters offer this protection—it's like a little bit of a mask—that lets you be out there and talk to your friends and be part of that culture," enjoying the positives of digital engagement while minimizing the risks that come with hypervisibility.

This isn't an abstract concern. Hess has written at length about her experiences as the target of online harassment and violent death threats. At times, her cyberstalkers incorporated her image into their abuse, commenting on her attractiveness (a common theme in harassment directed at women) and republishing it elsewhere alongside crude and vicious commentary. As much as women can be rewarded for putting their image out into the digital world, they're always at risk of being punished as well. Photo filters may not entirely shield us from that rage, but they can at least create a psychic barrier between those who wish us harm and ourselves.

If photo filters are a heightened form of the real-life beauty rituals women regularly engage in, the brutal harassment women are exposed to simply by existing online is, in a sense, an extreme form of the solicitations women endure when they leave their homes. Because as any woman who's gone to a bar, attended a party by herself, or even just walked down the street alone is well aware, merely existing in public as a woman is often treated as an explicit request for male attention—one even the most vocal discouragement is rarely able to dissuade.

There are no real-life Snapchat filters to protect women from the come-ons, the catcalls, and propositions they frequently endure. But there is another strategy that a woman can employ when she wants an interested man to leave her alone. It's just one that might involve being dishonest.

CHAPTER FIVE

I Have a Boyfriend

CRISTA ANNE GOT her first engagement ring when she was sixteen.

It wasn't anything fancy—just a bit of costume jewelry purchased at the Claire's in her local mall. And it hadn't actually been purchased for Anne by a fiancé—she'd bought it herself, using the discount she got as an employee at the Waldenbooks a few doors down. But to the men who patronized the bookstore, the ring served as a sign that she was off limits. And more than anything else that she might say or do to express her lack of interest in their expressions of interest and attraction, it acted as a deterrent to anyone thinking of hitting on her.

It's been almost twenty years since Anne worked at Waldenbooks, and in that time, she's found other creative ways to deflect the attentions of men. As she got older, the engagement ring evolved into a wedding ring; when she gained some weight, she started telling strange men that she wasn't just married, but pregnant as well. She's pretended to be deaf, using her basic knowledge of ASL to really sell the act; she's exaggerated the twitches and shakes caused by her Ehlers-Danlos syndrome and fibromyalgia to convince men she's too sick (or possibly too disturbed) to be desirable. Some of her theatrics have worked better than others, and sometimes they haven't worked at all. But Anne persists in spinning whatever fictions might render her unattractive and undesirable to men who attempt to hit on her. Because if there's one thing she's learned over the past few decades, it's that "I'm not interested" is almost never enough.

These fibs aren't unique to Anne: "I have a boyfriend" and its many variations are lies that've been told by countless women to countless men who don't seem to get the hint that their attentions are unwanted. If Anne's falsehoods are more extreme, or more creative, than those of the average woman, it's largely due to circumstance. During her years in Dallas, she relied on public transportation to get around—a reality that left her more vulnerable to the advances of strangers than women who could afford to travel by car. As a sex toy shop employee, she attracted the attention of men who assumed she'd be easy, slutty, or just more open to their advances. But even women who've never set foot on a subway, even women who don't know a thing about bondage or butt plugs, are familiar with the experience of men persisting in spite of obvious disinterest.

To some, these acts of dishonesty are just white lies women tell to protect male egos; to others, they're a more serious sign of a larger issue. When I ask Neil Strauss, author of *The Game: Penetrating the Secret Society of Pickup Artists*, he tells me he's never given the line much thought; regardless of whether a woman's boyfriend is real or imaginary, her rejection is ultimately feedback to learn from. Others are less sympathetic: a 2013 article that appeared on *xoJane* argued that women using this line are doing themselves— and their entire gender—a disservice, propping up male privilege by reinforcing the idea that a boyfriend (even a fake one) should carry more weight than a woman's lack of interest. The most extreme reaction I encountered was a viral prank—viewed millions of times on Facebook—by Brooklyn-based brothers Moe Bradberry and Etayyim Ray, which purports to out a woman who dares to lie about a nonexistent boyfriend, presenting itself as a public shaming that'll forever mark her with a scarlet L.

These deflections are so common that the rationale seems almost self-evident. Of course women lie: men don't listen to them. Of course women lie: it's the only way they can get some time to themselves. Yet taking this social strategy at face value means missing out on a much deeper story, one about how we teach men to pursue women, how we teach women to respond in kind, and what our ideas about romance and seduction reveal about being a woman in the world at large.

Around the time that Anne was buying her first engagement ring in an attempt to protect herself from men's advances, Arden Leigh was aggressively strategizing tactics to attract male attention and end her single streak. Leigh, the author of *The New Rules of Attraction: How to Get Him, Keep Him, and Make Him Beg for More* and founder of the Sirens Seduction Forum, doesn't seem like a woman who'd have trouble getting a date; indeed, during her years as a professional dominatrix, she quite literally had men paying for her time and attention.

But the enticing, seductive woman who welcomes me into her Los Angeles apartment is a creation of years of study and work. Throughout high school and college, Leigh was nerdy, awkward, and unsure how to attract love. She devoured books like *Why Men Love Bitches* and *The Rules*, which taught her that she'd secure a really great boyfriend by, as she puts it, "sitting still and being busy." But what she found instead was that the more she immersed herself in projects, the less men seemed to care. Frustrated by her chronic singledom, she decided to seek help from an unlikely source: the world of pickup artists, where men with names like Mystery and Matador experimented with different strategies for getting female attention, sharing their seduction skills with one another in an attempt to make it easier for men to get by in the dating world.[1]

"Here was this collective of men who were coming together who were—for better or worse—comparing strategies and really field testing their methods to get results. It was just incredibly results-oriented in a way that spoke to the logical part of my brain," Leigh tells me. It was a stark contrast to the dating advice being peddled to her own gender, which "tried to tell women that if you're being proactive, then you're just being clingy and desperate." Leigh felt that there had to be a way to give women the same strategic, results-oriented attitude toward dating, and so she immersed herself in the seduction community, studying pickup artist techniques and figuring out ways to reformulate them to meet the needs of women who are interested in dating men.

It's this background that's brought me to Leigh: I'm hoping that, as the rare woman who's spent significant time in the company of men who train other men how to pick up women, she'll have some insight into why it is, exactly, that men persist even in the face of a complete and total lack of interest.

"I often feel compassion for men," Leigh tells me as we drink tea in her Silver Lake living room, noting that the

---

[1] And, in the case of men who've made a career out of their pickup skills, to get rich as well.

burden of navigating and dictating the course of a romance is disproportionately seen as a male responsibility and that women aren't encouraged to make navigating the early stages of a romance easy. "Women are trained that if they say yes right away, they're sluts," Leigh notes. They're also discouraged from actively pursuing men, openly expressing sexual interest, or taking any assertive steps to advance their own romantic lives. Those dating guides that taught Leigh that being proactive was tantamount to being desperate? They also dissuaded women from starting conversations with men or taking an active role in advancing a romantic exchange. And the data suggest that, decades after the publication of *The Rules*, those beliefs still run deep: a 2015 analysis from dating site OkCupid noted that—regardless of age, attractiveness, or even sexual orientation—women are much less likely than men to send the first message.[2]

Whether it's online, in a bar, or through cultural osmosis, men, Leigh tells me, are constantly getting the message that women won't make the first move and that even when they're interested, they have a vested interest in demurring as a way to protect their reputation. From a male perspective, it's sometimes hard to know the difference between playing hard to get and actual disinterest. When women are taught to demur and dissemble even when they *are* interested in a man, is it really so shocking that men might not be prepared to take every no as a hard-and-fast refusal?

The idea that women who automatically say yes to a romantic advance are slutty, desperate, or otherwise overeager

---

[2] In my own dating life, I've repeatedly bucked this trend—though, interestingly, the patterns are so deeply ingrained that I've had men tell me to my face that they were the ones who initiated contact with me, even as our communications record proved that to be untrue.

for male attention is, Leigh tells, me, "so pervasive in our culture." It fuels the romantic tension and hijinks of rom coms; it pervades advice columns; it plays out in the dynamics of who initiates conversations on dating apps; it leads to arbitrary rules about how long we should wait to act on mutual sexual attraction and interest. And, at least in Leigh's eyes, it undergirds the dynamic of male persistence that women find so aggravating. "That's honestly where a lot of pickup comes from: being persistent enough that a woman has an excuse to say, 'It just happened'"—"it," of course, being sex. While that persistence may, at times, lead to unwanted, overly aggressive come-ons, it's a strategy that makes sense in a society where women are actively punished for being open and honest about their sexual desires. As Leigh sums up the situation, "You can't blame women for saying no when they mean yes, but you can't then blame men for believing that a woman's no could actually be a yes that she needs to just not feel slutty about."

Pickup artists, Leigh tells me, have a number of strategies for pushing through hesitation and getting a woman to let her guard down. If a woman responds to an invitation by claiming to have a boyfriend, for instance, an easy rejoinder is to let her know that her boyfriend's not invited to join the fun. "Honestly, it would be a bad thing if it were not for the fact that some women who are lying about saying they have a boyfriend...just need to feel more attraction or connection with this guy before they're like, 'You know, actually I don't have a boyfriend,'" Leigh remarks. It's a troubling sentiment that's similar to one that's been communicated to me, time and again, by male friends. Every story I tell about men who refuse to believe me when I say I don't want something, who ignore my boundaries and assume interest where none exists, seems to be met with a tale of "some girls" who aren't straightforward about their desires, who won't communicate what they want, who need men to take the lead and push things forward and help the relationship progress—as though the existence of women who can't communicate justifies ignoring the will of those who can.

Even Leigh, who's literally made a career out of being straightforward about her romantic interests, has found that expectations of female demurral affect how men react to her. Over the course of our conversation, she tells me about the various men who've pushed up against her boundaries. There've been polyamorous men who've assumed that her mere presence within the community automatically indicated an interest in sex with anyone who might offer. A sex therapist who met her disinterest with an overt attempt at persuasion. And, in a particularly frustrating tale, an author who announced on a third date that he was "really starting to take [her] at [her] word"—as though it somehow requires weeks of demonstrated honesty for a woman to actually be trusted.

But in spite of these negative experiences, Leigh still retains a surprising amount of sympathy for men, significantly more than I'm able to muster. Leigh believes that it's bad programming, more than bad intent, that leads to the exchanges that women like Anne find so off-putting. In her view, if men had a better understanding of what women went through, if women were more forthright about their desires, we all might be a bit better off. In an attempt to illustrate how this might work, Leigh introduces me to the concept of "bitch shield," a bit of pickup artist terminology that, she stresses to me, is far more compassionate than the name might suggest. Rather than an attempt to denigrate women, she tells me, it's actually about teaching men that "women get approached so often, especially if they're attractive, that they would rather be rude to you than give you their time." The ultimate lesson here is that men can't take rejection personally; if they want to succeed in pickup, they need to figure out a way to make themselves worthy of a woman's time.

And yet despite her optimism about the power of teaching men to approach women with empathy rather than aggression, Leigh is fully aware that—whatever its compassionate intent—the mere notion of bitch shield "sometimes means that people who follow that train of thought don't always honor a woman's no," assuming that rejection is just a defense that needs to be broken down. It's that thin line between persistence and harassment that seems to be the crux of the issue. For every woman I know, that line is a glaring, obvious, and readily apparent one. Yet for some reason, men either can't—or don't want to—see it.

In order to understand male persistence, JT Tran tells me, I have to develop a deeper understanding of heterosexual attraction. "What is the most attractive thing about a man that you would want to date?" he asks me.

"Someone I can have a good conversation with," I reply. That seems to throw him for a second, but he quickly recovers. Most women, he tells me, are looking for a confident man—and what is confidence if not persisting in the face of negativity?

Tran, it should be noted, was not always confident. In his early twenties, he was a smart, successful rocket scientist, one with a place on the beach and a shiny new Mercedes— and yet, he tells me, "I sucked at dating." Society had told him that women would flock to him if he just achieved enough, but despite his many successes, he faced rejection after rejection. Even eHarmony rejected him, he tells me, noting that he was "too cerebral."

Like Leigh, Tran turned to the pickup community to solve his dating woes; like Leigh, he eventually shifted his personal interest in pickup into a professional one, founding a dating coach company called The ABCs of Attraction.[3] It is, he tells me, more than pickup tips: instead of just teaching clients how to get results in the dating scene, Tran's company focuses on teaching them how to have a well-rounded, healthy lifestyle and relationship.

"I always tell my guys that if you can think from a woman's perspective, you'll be better off," he tells me. In his prepickup days, he'd assume that a woman who rejected him was "a bitch, a lesbian, or a racist," but in the years since, he's come to understand that the bitch shield is just a defense mechanism employed by women who are constantly fending off the unwanted attention of men. Developing a fan base, Tran tells me, made him particularly sympathetic to the plight of hot women: while being approached by strangers who want to talk to you can, at times, be fun, it's equally likely to be scary. At a hotel in Sydney, Tran was chased down by a fan. Even as a man, he found the experience frightening; if he were a woman, he tells me, it likely would have been terrifying.

Yet even with this rudimentary empathy, Tran's confidence in the power—and *necessity*—of confidence is unshakeable. I ask him about a particularly noxious bit of

---

[3] At Tran's explicit request, I'm letting you know his company's website is abcsofattraction.com.

dating advice I'd watched go viral: a blog post from pickup coach the Modern Man titled "How to Talk to a Woman Wearing Headphones." At first, he seems amenable to my perspective, noting that he's aware that "girls put on headphones distinctly to avoid talking to people, I understand that." But as his train of thought continues, it begins to stray away from empathy for the woman who just wants to be left alone: "If women didn't want confident men, that shouldn't be a prerequisite for dating."

For Tran, the question is less, "Should men leave women alone?" and more "Can a man figure out how to approach a strange woman—even one clearly indicating she doesn't want to talk to someone—in a way she'll ultimately appreciate?" If an approach is done properly, he tells me, it can be really fun, really enjoyable—so much so that even a woman who thought she didn't want to be approached will be better off for the experience.

"Initially, maybe she doesn't really want to talk to the guy, but all of a sudden this really fun guy comes into her world and sweeps her off her feet," he says. "I mean, I don't know a single girl that's like, 'No, I don't ever want to be swept off my feet. I just want to live a really boring life.' I think everybody kind of wants those magical movie moments where things click and you have a really positive interaction with a guy."

I can understand the appeal of this explanation, the fantasy of that perfect pickup that seems straight out of a romantic comedy. But there's an inherent problem to Tran's logic, one that is immediately apparent to me but he seems oblivious to. Of course women might make an exception for a truly magical experience, for a man who's really, truly worth it, but if every man convinces himself that he's the exception, the one for whom it's okay to talk to a woman with headphones on, to ignore a woman's profession of disinterest, the exception ceases to be exceptional.

I think back on the many times strange men have approached me, unbidden, on the streets of New York. The men who've approached me as I waited for a friend, striking up conversations as I stood outside a café examining my phone. The men who've proposed marriage at first sight. The man who, yes, encouraged me to take off my headphones just so he could inform me that we'd been sitting on the subway together a few minutes earlier. Maybe these men thought they were being clever; maybe they thought they were creating special, magical moments. To me, though, they were a series of annoyances, a ceaseless parade of interrupting men creating a nonstop hum of unmemorable approaches. It's a tragedy of the commons, with women bearing the brunt of the tragic burden.

"Pepé Le Pew was my first example of a harasser," says Debjani Roy, deputy director of Hollaback, a global grassroots movement to end harassment. The Warner Bros. creation—an amorous skunk who aggressively pursues the affections of a cat, undeterred by her obvious disinterest—isn't exactly presented as a romantic hero. But he's not a villain either. It's supposed to be comical that he's oblivious to the way his foul scent renders him unappealing, that, like Wile E. Coyote, he persists in his goal in spite of repeated failure. His over-the-top seduction act may never be successful, but we're nonetheless supposed to be charmed by the lovestruck skunk. His confidence is intended, after a fashion, to win the audience over—even as it drives the object of his affection away.

And while it may be tempting to write Le Pew off as nothing more than an outdated relic of antiquated attitudes[4] toward dating and seduction, it's worth noting that the assumptions that underlie Le Pew's pursuit aren't all that different from those that shape the dating guidelines that Leigh and Tran alternately combat and reinforce. The notion that women can't or won't be aggressive about their desires, the idea that male confidence is the ultimate aphrodisiac—all this is on display within Le Pew's adventures, which normalize and reinforce these ideas of gendered behavior for the children who consume the cartoons as entertainment. Le Pew doesn't read silence, or evasiveness, or even aggression as rejection, because he exists in a world where women are expected to be coy, to play hard to get, to put up a shield until they're sufficiently persuaded to engage. And, more than seventy years after Le Pew's debut, those assumptions about female behavior are still very much in effect.

The scenario that plays out in a Le Pew cartoon is also the scenario that plays out in a number of romantic comedies, that is embedded into our love songs and every aspect of our pop culture. When Tran tells me women want a confident partner, this is what he's actually saying. We're conditioned to think of it as normal when a man persists in professing his affections and desires in spite of repeated rejection; we're supposed to find it romantic, admirable, and even sweet when a man aggressively attempts to woo an unwilling woman into a sexual relationship. Numerous romantic comedies rely on the trope of "the woman doesn't like the man and the man is pursuing, and the audience is rooting

---

[4] Or, perhaps, not so outdated: in July 2016, director Max Landis announced that he'd be penning a Pepé Le Pew movie.

for this to happen," notes *The Game* author Strauss; we're culturally conditioned to see male persistence as an admirable quality to be encouraged, not an abusive behavior that should be condemned.

The trope is unbelievably common. It's in comedies like the original *Ghostbusters* and romances like *Gone with the Wind*, as well as rom coms like *Ten Things I Hate About You* (itself a modern update of Shakespeare's *Taming of the Shrew*).[5] Holiday classics like "Baby It's Cold Outside" and R&B hits like Chris Brown's "Yo (Excuse Me Miss)" both position persuading an uninterested woman as the height of romance. The message that male desire trumps female resistance, that obsessive persistence is not just admirable but romantic, is already a troubling and problematic one. But what makes it even more insidious is that we're so rarely presented with an alternative perspective or view.

"In culture, the male voice or experience is the universalized one. So of course that's the 'true' one," Jessica Valenti, the founder of feminist blog Feministing, tells me. "If you don't even have an example of a female voice talking about what [women] want ever, then the only one that exists is the male one, so of course [men] listen to it and believe it." Individual women may say that, for instance, they're perfectly capable of expressing their romantic desires, that they don't find persistence charming, that they aren't looking to be won over by an aggressively confident man. But when the dominant narrative is saying otherwise, and when that dominant narrative lines up with a situation that's favorable to men, there's little incentive to disbelieve it. By

---

[5] In a particularly noxious example, *Revenge of the Nerds* presents a sexual assault as a romantic meet cute.

reinforcing this narrative of feminine passivity and masculine aggression, we help train men to see their desire—and not a woman's consent—as the ultimate arbiter of any potential romantic or sexual situation.

"I eventually find myself talking to one of the girls that Tom handed a beer to....I thought me and her were enjoying each other's company, when she got up close to me and said that she was astonished that I looked exactly like one of her friends at the school that she went to. I took this as a sign that she was flirting with me."

This is how Brock Turner, a Stanford student found guilty of three felony counts of sexual assault, describes meeting his victim in a statement he submitted to the court. Turner—whom two witnesses found fingering an unconscious woman, who lay half naked behind a dumpster—is an obvious outlier in the spectrum of sexual behavior, but the narrative he weaves, one in which he repeatedly talks of assuming and rationalizing and thinking things were going fine, isn't all that different from the way most men talk about their romantic and sexual pursuits. Turner talks about his victim as a person whose consent was apparent because he, and he alone, perceived it to exist; because he interpreted her behavior in a way that suggested she wanted sex, then clearly that interest was real. It didn't matter that she was blackout drunk, that she didn't vocalize her consent, that there was no way she *could* have expressed consent. Turner desired her and assumed he could manifest her consent in response.

In her memoir, *Sex Object*, Jessica Valenti encapsulates what it feels like to be on the receiving end of this sort of one-sided romance. In the essay "D," Valenti writes of an email she received from a married friend, a man whose sons go on play dates with her daughter, that expresses his interest in fucking her—an interest, he notes, that's persisted for almost a year. Valenti's take on the moment that sparked this man's lust reads as follows:

> I was wearing a crop top and a high-waisted skirt, so that a small sliver of my upper waist showed. I was glad to be out of the house and glad [my daughter] was spending the night with a babysitter so [my husband] and I could have a fun night out in a city that we didn't know all that well.
>
> A few drinks into the party, I snuck out with D to have a cigarette. . . . While we talked, he briefly put his hand on the exposed part of my waist. He stood closer than he should have and said we should sneak out for cigarettes more often. He had always been a flirt. . . . D is well-known in his field and good-looking. But he is not someone who oozes sexuality. I was not remotely interested.

Valenti, like so many women, blames herself for this exchange, assuming that she somehow courted her friend's attention by giving off some unintentionally welcoming vibe, by presenting herself as open to an extramarital affair, by not shutting down his flirtations quickly enough. Surely, she thinks, there must have been something about her actions, about *her*, that invited this proposition—yet it's equally if not more likely that her friend merely felt desire, then told himself that she had invited it.

When I ask Valenti about this experience, she agrees that "there definitely was this narrative in his head versus a much different narrative in mine." Valenti had seen flirtation—even flirtation bordering on impropriety—as utterly unremarkable, just part and parcel of how men approach women. But for D, her continued friendliness, even in the absence of any expression of interest, was enough to constitute an indication that she wanted him to take his flirtation further.

When women are assumed to be unable, or unwilling, to overtly communicate desire, men treat everything as a covert expression of desire, a secret code that they and they alone have the power to decipher. If a woman is wearing jeans, if she's walking down a certain street, if she's dressed in a way that a man finds attractive—all of this is, presumably, a way of signaling romantic interest. If women tolerate a come-on, it's a clear sign that it's wanted (a particularly frustrating read given how routinely women are socialized to be polite). In the worldview constructed by men, if women didn't want to be approached by amorous strangers, they wouldn't dress in an appealing way, or go out drinking in bars, or, I suppose, even leave their homes.

And—like Valenti analyzing her behavior to determine what she might have done to lead her friend on—women struggle to adapt in response, attempting to figure out what they can do that will adequately communicate their lack of interest. Hollaback director Roy describes a "sartorial edit" that women often engage in before leaving the house: the attempt to figure out which outfit, which shoes, which makeup and hairstyle will allow them to move through life without courting unwanted attention. Even when they *are* trying to attract potential partners, it feels necessary to strike the perfect balance: to craft a sexy, not slutty, ensemble that advertises interest without declaring open season on their sexual availability.

Valenti describes the phenomenon as "constantly looking for those open doors that you need to close," noting that women are self-police to make sure that nothing they do could be construed as sexual availability. For many men, she says, "the default is not, this person is not interested in me and let me see if they are, the default is, of course this person is interested in me.... It's a yes until it's a no, as opposed to the opposite."

Yet more often than not, women's actions and adaptations don't matter. "[Men's] reading of the situation prevails," Roy notes. It's not merely that men's views are given more weight; when a man describes how a sexual situation unfolds, in many people's eyes, "that *is* the narrative. Anything else is confusing, or untrue, or worthy of disdain." It's embedded in the insistence that men know what women really want, that harassment is actually complimentary, that women who accuse men of assault were asking for it or being flirtatious or somehow, in some way, actually giving consent.

I'm brought back, again, to Tran's insistence that women want to be swept off their feet, that any intrusion can ultimately be consensual so long as it's done correctly. When you exist in a world where the greatest compliment that can be paid to women is male attention, then it's easy to believe that the only problem is approaching women incorrectly, or approaching women who are already taken—and not that aggressively, relentlessly approaching women might be the issue in and of itself.

As much as I want to buy into the idea that this all just a matter of good intentions gone awry, it feels naive to paint male aggression as merely the result of misguided dating advice that's been amplified by stereotypes and gendered expectations. It is difficult to assume good faith when a man assumes that a woman in a committed same-sex relationship is eager to open up her bedroom to a lascivious straight male gaze. It is difficult to assume good faith when coming out as bisexual is automatically viewed as an invitation to a three-way. It is difficult to assume good faith when even an imaginary boyfriend—or, stunningly, the physical presence of a real one—isn't enough to deter the pursuit; when a woman sitting next to her massive Marine boyfriend finds a strange man pulling up her shirt to get a better look at her tattoo.

It's Bella Vendetta, a stripper based in western Massachusetts, who shares these stories with me. Over the years, she's dealt with her fair share of male persistence; these days, she says, she can't even go out for a drink with her girlfriend without getting harassed by men. "My girlfriend doesn't lie," Vendetta tells me. "She just tells people, 'I'm gay,'" assuming that her queerness will deflect any further sexual attention. "It never does," Vendetta says; to the contrary, the men they run into see this declaration of identity as a challenge. "They spend the rest of the night trying to convince her that she's not gay, and that she just needs a man."

The night before our conversation, Vendetta had been out for drinks with friends; instead of being able to relax and enjoy a beer, she'd spent much of the night fending off the attentions of a group of construction workers who figured they'd charm—or badger—their way into getting some sexual attention from a hot stripper and her girlfriend. The anecdote—which ended with Vendetta finally getting some peace when the men moved on to a more welcoming woman[6]—might have been entertaining if it were an

---

[6] One who, to Vendetta's amusement, hustled them for drinks all night and then went home with another guy.

isolated occurrence. But the experience of being relentlessly pursued by men who are convinced that with enough effort they'll find their way into her pants is so common it's practically become background noise to Vendetta's experience of womanhood.

The approaches men use on her are, she tells me, rather familiar: they're along the lines of a less skilled version of the hard sell she uses on men during her work as a stripper. "When I go into a regular club or a bar, and dudes are trying to hit on me, it's like, 'You're using the same tactics that I use to try to get money out of people, except you're trying to get sex out of me,'" she tells me. But while it's reasonable for a stripper to assume that every man who enters her place of business is consenting to be a part of a transactional relationship—that he is, in essence, volunteering to be approached and pitched to simply by walking through a strip club's doors—it's vastly different for a man to assume that any woman he comes across—any woman who goes out for a drink, who goes out dancing, who dares to leave her home—is de facto consenting to being sexually pursued. It's one thing to be treated like a mark in one specific, discrete area of life that you can easily avoid if you prefer. It's wholly another to be treated that way every time you go out into the world.

And yet perhaps we shouldn't be surprised. Roy, for one, isn't shocked by the similarities that Vendetta's noticed between these seemingly unrelated encounters. "The whole dynamic that's happening around street harassment is obviously a power imbalance," she tells me. "There's an element of ownership over public spaces—who owns that street." A stripper aggressively pursues a patron because he's in her workplace and thus owes her money; harassment can be considered men's way of announcing to women, "This is my space, this is my street, and you're inhabiting my space for this moment."

It may seem odd to position the street—or bars, or public transportation, or any public environment where women are forced to fend off unwanted attention—as a male-owned space, but it's worth considering that, in the most literal of all senses, the infrastructures of our cities were explicitly designed for men. In a 1980 essay titled "What Would a Non-Sexist City Be Like? Speculations on Housing, Urban Design, and Human Work," Dolores Hayden opens by remarking that "'A woman's place is in the home' has been one of the most important principles of architectural design and urban planning in the United States for the last century." Though Hayden is largely preoccupied with looking at how urban design and zoning have helped to keep women out of the workforce and in the kitchen, there's an unspoken inverse to her argument. If private spaces are the domain of women, then public spaces are the domain of men[7]—and any woman who ventures into a male domain must, on some level, be interested in or even explicitly asking for male attention.

Early saloons often banned women, many public transportation systems were initially designed with commuting men in mind, and, of course, the idea that a woman traveling unaccompanied is not merely acceptable but unremarkable is a relatively new one within American culture. So many of the spaces we currently see as open to all genders were not originally fashioned that way—and it shouldn't

---

[7] In some areas of the world, this dynamic plays out quite literally: take, for instance, Saudi Arabia, where until recently women were not allowed to drive, and guardianship laws greatly restrict their movement outside the home.

come as a surprise that women are, as a result, often treated more like an invasive species or a form of entertainment than native inhabitants who have as much right to take up space as their male counterparts do.

"Women's attitudes [about] being in public spaces have shifted much more quickly than a lot of straight men are able to understand or to acknowledge," Roy notes. A number of studies have backed up this assertion: young men consistently lag behind their female peers when it comes to attitudes about the role of women in the workplace and the domestic sphere. Millennial men are still uncomfortable with the idea of female leaders, still assume that women should do the majority of domestic labor, and, most disappointingly, are the group most likely to say that feminist progress has gone far enough. This disparity creates a stunning clash in gendered expectations: women my age grew up with the promise that we could be anyone, or anything, we desired, while our male peers were still raised to expect the same degree of privilege, power, and female submission they'd always been afforded. As a result, women enter the adult world and are shocked to discover that it hasn't quite adapted to accommodate their full personhood— and men are shocked, and sometimes angered, to discover women don't want to accommodate their desires.

"What I struggle with is that even as new generations come up who are living and existing amongst new ways of being and envisioning what relationships should look like, a lot of men haven't necessarily cared to understand or adapt," Roy begins. Then her tone abruptly changes, taking on a hint of bitterness. "Why should they? They're in a position of power where they feel like they can dictate the rules of how everything goes."

And perhaps, she muses, the harassment women face is a panicked reaction to a fear that men might be losing that position of power. "If there's no one on the other end who's responding to [an expression of dominance], it's clearly un-successful. And then you have a bunch of very frustrated people." What we see on the streets, she surmises, is "a lot of frustration of men not fully understanding what their role is anymore. With that comes a level of persistence, and with that comes escalation and with that comes violence."

Valenti also sees a connection between feminist progress and increased male persistence and aggression. As women's voices become louder and more prominent, she tells me, men are being exposed to a perspective wholly unlike the one they've known their whole lives. And, she surmises, the fact that these perspectives "feel so unfamiliar, that is where some of the disbelief comes in." Because the perspective women offer—that they aren't constantly interested in and open to male attention, that they don't want to be relentlessly pursued, that they would like to be left alone sometimes—is so radically different from what men are used to hearing, "it feels instinctively untrue." And as a result, it must be rejected aggressively and sometimes violently.

Viewing male sexual aggression and persistence as a power struggle and a display of dominance as much as—if not more than—a genuine romantic appeal makes the boy-friend lie an even more obvious strategy for a woman eager to extricate herself from an uncomfortable situation. If it's male power that matters here, then only the presence of an-other man—imaginary though he might be—can adequately push back against unwanted attention. "A woman as an indi-vidual isn't necessarily seen as a separate entity or a person who has a life, agency, desire," Roy tells me. What women want isn't the central question; it's what role they play in the lives of men that matters more than anything. Creating an imaginary man to deflect the desires and attention of other men isn't so much a lie, Roy offers. "It's really a survival strategy."

And as survival strategies go, "I have a boyfriend" is one that manages to effectively assert disinterest while sparing the male ego and adhering to traditional ideas of who wields power in both public spaces and private relationships. It's imperfect, of course—critics are right to note that by appealing to an imaginary boyfriend, women are upholding the idea that male ownership matters more than female agency—but when you're fending off a harasser, it can be hard to hold on to your high-minded ideals.

Crista Anne does have an alternative strategy for women who are loathe to rely on a fictional boyfriend, however. "I will scare [men] off by hitting on them twice as hard and throwing that degrading language right back at them. They come at me like, 'I bet your tits feel great'? 'I bet your cock is huge; I can't wait to feel it throbbing against me.' Boom, gone." It's a tactic with obvious risks, but at least it's one that allows women to claim power for themselves rather than ceding it to some made-up male authority figure.

"Maybe it just comes down to, 'What is the way you think of other people?' Are you thinking of them as human beings with needs that are equal to your own, or are you thinking of them as objects?" Neil Strauss says to me. "You can do all the right things, but if your belief is that you're using someone as an object, that becomes problematic."

It should go without saying that most women are accustomed to being viewed as objects. It is part and parcel of the way they are sexualized, the way they are positioned as prizes to be won, the way they are discussed as conquests, the way they are framed in relation to the men in their lives—as daughters, as girlfriends, as wives, as mothers—before they are ever seen as individual human beings. More troublingly, this status as objects doesn't end at the boundaries of public life; oftentimes, it persists into our intimate relationships, as women fight to be seen as unique, individual people, rather than madonnas or whores whose actions can be conveniently slotted into some predetermined script.

Which may explain why, for many women, the lying doesn't cease when they enter into a relationship—even (and sometimes especially) one with someone they really, truly adore.

Strauss notes that lies can be roughly divided into one of two categories. There are the lies we tell out of politeness, to spare someone's feelings, and there are lies we tell to uphold and adhere to a social fiction we'll be punished for transgressing. Most of us assume that the lies that women tell their partners fall into the former category, but I'd argue that, just as often, these lies are of the latter type. Yes, women lie to their partners about their sexual pasts to protect those partner's egos, to boost their confidence in the belief that they're the best and most talented lovers ever. But women also lie to their partners about their sexual pasts to uphold the notion that they've stuck to the societally sanctioned script, that they've earned their happy ending—and that no one has the right to try to take it away.

CHAPTER SIX

I've Never Done This Before

GROWING UP, AUTUMN didn't see a lot of women who looked like her on TV. And when she did, their depictions often made her uncomfortable: the few black women represented in the shows she saw "were loud or aggressive or really, really sexual. You'd have the prim white girls and the quiet Asians and the loud, sassy black women and the sassy Hispanics. All that I saw was that I was supposed to be really sexual."

That wasn't the kind of woman Autumn wanted to be—but everywhere she went, she got the message that this stereotype was exactly what the world expected from her. "I started having people be sexual to me because of my race when I was twelve," she tells me over the phone. "[Adult men] knew how old I was, but they would still be like, 'Oh I got that jungle fever—I hear that black women really know how to do X, Y, Z.'"

As a teenager, Autumn did everything she could to avoid being seen as a sexual being ("I didn't masturbate until I was nineteen years old," she tells me). But as she got older, playing the role of the prim and proper good girl got increasingly tiresome. She began to date, exploring sex and relationships—and, disappointingly, discovered that all the expectations and stereotypes she'd been trying to avoid were still in full force.

There is, Autumn tells me, a recurring trend among the men she pursues. "They're interested in me only if they think that they're the first time that I've done anything," she says, noting that she routinely downplays her sexual experience, reducing her partner count of nine to just one or two, or denying that she's engaged in anything but the most vanilla sex acts. When she doesn't, she tells me, "[Men] think I've had so much sex that they don't have to be attached to me—they can see it as a fling and not have to worry about me or how I feel about it."

And yet as much as the men she's met profess an interest in relatively virginal women, they paradoxically want partners with the skill set of someone with years of sexual experience. "They expect me to know how to do all the kinky stuff," she tells me. "They expect me to know how they want it, when they want it. They expect me to know exactly what I'm doing when it comes to anything, *anything* involving sex," she says. "If I openly admit that I have experience with it, I'm a slut, but if I somehow magically know how to do it without saying anything beforehand, I'm the best."

It is, perhaps, an update on the virgin/whore dichotomy, one in which women are somehow expected to inhabit both states at the exact same time. "People expect you to be this perpetually pure snowflake and have no experience, but then when you get into having sex, they demand that you have this long list of sexual experiences," Autumn explains. "'I want you to be really pure, but you have to give really good head.' It's impossible."

Autumn isn't the only woman who's noticed this pattern. According to Charlotte Shane, author of the memoir *Prostitute Laundry* and a retired sex worker, our current sexual ideal is a woman who "is not modest, who's incredibly eager actually, really 'adventurous.' She has this insatiable enthusiasm for sex," as well as an expansive, impressive knowledge of how to bring her partner to the height of sexual pleasure. But, Shane notes, men "don't want to have to think about how she got that knowledge." In a similar vein, Rachel Hills, author of *The Sex Myth*, tells me that "women feel like they should be sexually experienced, they shouldn't be virgins, but that they shouldn't have too many sexual partners either.... There's a premium on being adventurous and trying new things, but on the other hand, a lot of men are afraid of things that women are told we should be doing. Be kinky but not too kinky. Don't be boring, but don't freak men out."

If all those qualifications are making your head spin, you're not alone. Women are accustomed to being presented with punishing, difficult standards that they're expected to somehow effortlessly live up to, but the parameters placed on their sexual histories are literally impossible to achieve. Is it any wonder that, like Autumn, a number of women have discovered that it's just easier to lie?

"Nobody can play a violin the first time they pick it up," sex advice columnist Dan Savage tells me over the phone. "But we're expected to play a human being the first time we pick one of those up. And play it expertly." And humans—with our complicated sexual response systems that require the coordination of both our physical and our emotional side in order to achieve the peak of pleasure—are "a lot more complicated than just a violin, which is just some catgut on a stick."

Through Savage Love, his widely syndicated column, Savage has popularized the notion that all of us should strive to be GGG—or good in bed, giving "equal time and equal pleasure" to one's partner, and game "for anything—within reason." But being good at sex, he tells me, "requires some practice," and the idea that sexual expertise should be effortless, spontaneous, and inborn is a deeply damaging one.

And yet it's an idea that's incredibly widespread. It's in films in which couples fall into passionate embraces without a murmur of discussion about what each of them does and doesn't like, where wordless passion is presented as the height of romanticism. It's in romance novels in which fantasy lovers know exactly what they want without ever having to be asked, and in porn movies in which the hours of communication, preparation, and negotiation are edited out of the final product (or, more likely, never even committed to film). The trope is so omnipresent it's hard to say where, exactly, it got its start—though Savage, who was raised Catholic, suspects that sex-negative religions might have played some part. "If you're going to sin, sin once," he quips, noting that the idea that thinking about sex is as sinful as actually doing it encourages us to pretend that we "got swept away" rather than acknowledging that good, enjoyable sex is something that takes planning, premeditation, and communication.

Even if you're not worried that some all-powerful being is going to strike you down for thinking smutty thoughts, it's hard to escape the notion that sex is something we should be good at from the very first time, that it should just come naturally in the moment, as though the same hormones that cause lubrication and erection also send our brain a step-by-step script for how to bring our partner the most pleasure. Arriving at sex unsure of how to proceed is shameful, embarrassing, and to be avoided. But how, exactly, is a person supposed to be skilled at the sex they've never even had? How is a woman supposed to know exactly how to do a thing she's never done before?

"When I was younger, I thought, 'I'll read every book that's ever been written on sexual technique and that will make me a genius,'" Charlotte Shane tells me, laughing as she relates this anecdote. "Which of course is one of the worst things I can think to do to someone: give them a stack of sexual how tos and be like, 'You're a savant now.'" Because so long as being "good" in bed is defined as more than a mere willingness to spread one's legs and be penetrated, it's impossible to develop any kind of sexual expertise without a bit of real-world trial and error. Yes, scores of books offer point-by-point breakdowns of what a blow job is supposed to entail, or what sexual positions ensure the most pleasurable experience, but the gap between reading about something and actually being good at it is vast indeed.

Not even porn flicks—which obviously offer more, and more explicit, detail than a book could ever provide—are enough to turn someone into a sexual master. Assuming, first and foremost, that the porn movie you're enjoying even depicts a kind of sex you're interested in and actually capable of engaging in, there's the pesky fact that most porn movies are fantasies that obscure essential details from the viewing audience, neglecting to show how best to prepare for anal sex, or what important safety guidelines were set up before the performers kicked off a scene of extreme kink. Even educational porn films, which are far more likely to showcase all of the preparation that goes into effortless-seeming sex, are just instructional videos, not magical, automatic transfers of knowledge and skill. We don't expect a knitting tutorial to instantly transform a viewer into an expert crafter.

"How do you get good at anything else?" Shane asks me. "You don't read all the books on biking and then go compete in the Tour de France." Although the idea that books alone could transform someone into a master of all things in sex is one that Shane finds "funny and sweet," it also points to a deeper truth that she finds incredibly troubling. Embedded in the idea that sexual knowledge should be acquired through nonsexual means is the suggestion that the only sex worth having is the kind that's already perfect—that coming to your partner with a desire to experiment, explore, or develop a new skill is somehow shameful and to be avoided at all costs.

And, of course, there's the implication that anyone whose skills were acquired through the vast field test known as "sleeping around" is to be avoided at all costs. Or would be, if we could collectively agree on what, exactly, counts as sleeping around.

Since writing *The Sex Myth*, Rachel Hills has devoted herself to debunking the idea that there's a particular way we should all be having sex—though the college audiences she gives talks to aren't always as receptive as she'd like. At a recent talk, she tells me, "one young woman raised her hand and said, 'What's the right number of partners to have?' ... I told her there was no right number of partners, and that was not a satisfactory answer."

It's not surprising that many of us still buy into the idea that there's a specific number of sexual partners that will guarantee everlasting happiness. It's a message that we're bombarded with over and over again—though there never seems to be any agreement on what the appropriate number of sex partners actually is. In December 2016, the *Daily Mail* reported on a study conducted by three UK universities that put forth three as the "magic number" for both men and women; not even five months later, that very same paper reported twelve as the ideal and nineteen as the upper limit—though tellingly, these latter numbers came not from a scientific study, but a survey produced by an adultery-themed dating website. Men frequently hold women to a more exacting standard than women hold other women to: when men are making the call, Hills tells me, "Two or three is the right number. One might also be acceptable, but zero is bad and five is bad." In contrast, the romantic comedy *What's Your Number?*—written by two women, and based on a book by a third—is far more generous: a woman can bed up to twenty partners before she's rendered incapable of finding true love.

Though the number itself may change, the sentiment behind a fixed, "ideal" number of sexual partners remains fairly consistent. Women want enough sexual experience to prove they know what they're doing but not so much that they wind up permanently labeled as an oversexed slut. It's a slightly more realistic goal than attempting to be a virgin who gives a killer blow job and is proficient in all manner of depraved and exotic kinks, but it's still rather opaque, particularly when no one can actually agree on what that magic number is. The most telling advice I found on the topic came from Hills, who related that one of the women she'd interviewed for her book declared that men want women to have "the same number of [sex] partners as you've had boyfriends. You can maybe have one or two more, but if the number of partners is much more than that, it relegates you to slut territory."

That allegedly ideal connection between number of sex partners and number of relationships offers a bit of clarity as to what we're actually trying to communicate when we talk about a woman's number. "Something we look for in partners is good judgment," Dan Savage tells me. "We read good or bad judgment in all sorts of actions that people make," including, for instance, one's willingness to engage in casual sex and one-night stands. The higher a person's number, the more it's assumed that they're a wild, risk-taking sort of person. But the correlation between our "number" and the conditions under which we had sex is rarely a straightforward one—a reality that, somewhat fittingly, was best illustrated by HBO's long-running sitcom *Sex and the City*.

In the lead-up to the first *Sex and the City* movie, the staff of the *New York Daily News* took an analytical look at the series, calculating that over the course of six seasons the four central characters had bedded a total of ninety-five partners. The bulk of those hookups were, unsurprisingly, credited to libertine Samantha, but even chaste, prim Charlotte had bedded eighteen different men.[1] On paper that number may seem imposing—especially considering that, as a woman in her thirties, Charlotte presumably had a decade of sexual experience prior to the show's six seasons—but over the course

---

[1] Carrie tied with Charlotte; Miranda pulled up the rear with seventeen sex partners.

of the series, it all feels rather natural. Eighteen partners over six years averages out to just three per year. As Charlotte bounces from serious relationship to casual fling to hopefully serious relationship that fizzles far too quickly, it's easy to see how she acquires a supposedly formidable number of sex partners.

The context around our sexual experiences is often much more telling than the naked number alone. Whatever her "number" might suggest about her morality, Charlotte still perceives herself as a traditional, relatively conservative woman—and in all the ways that matter, she is. Charlotte may have sex with (slightly) more men than modern, ambitious Miranda, but she's still the one who prioritizes motherhood over career, who opts to be a stay-at-home mom, who privileges the needs of her family over her own needs—all the things that, of course, a "slutty" woman is supposedly incapable of doing.

And this concept of a traditionally minded, socially conservative "good" girl who nevertheless racks up her fair share of sexual conquests isn't just the stuff of fiction. The woman who told Hills that a woman's number of past sexual partners should equal her number of past relationships was a conservative Republican, one whose good-girl exterior stood in sharp contrast to the sexually voracious woman she happened to be in private. According to Hills, the woman managed these contradictory sides of herself by only pursuing sex in the context of a relationship—and, as a result, immediately starting a new relationship as soon as one ended. She may have had a lot of sex, but it was always in the context of a relationship—a significant detail entirely obscured when considering her "number" alone.

The number of people we've had sex with is just one limited data point in our sexual history, one that, stripped of context, reveals far less than we think. That knowledge can shape the way women choose to quantify and frame their sexual histories. Savage tells me that women who write to him often manufacture "a number that doesn't count just oral sex or doesn't count a three-way or doesn't count an adventure that's crazily out of character—they only count relationships; they don't count one night stands. They want a smaller number so as not to stoke the insecurities of the guy that they're with"—and, one assumes, so as to accurately represent who they feel they *really* are as a sexual being.

Of course, all of this is based on the assumption that our sexual pasts actually reflect who we are in the present. And that's an assertion that's pretty debatable.

"How long does it take to have sex with a man?" Charlotte Shane asks me over lunch at a bistro in Chinatown. "News flash: not that long." If she were to proposition a stranger in the restaurant for a quickie in the bathroom, she tells me, "I could walk out five minutes later. *Five minutes*. Five minutes in one day. That's nothing! I spend more than five minutes a day pooping."

There's something almost childishly naive about our notion that a sexual experience is inherently transformative or that it creates a lasting bond, that that five minutes spent in flagrante delicto is automatically more meaningful than five minutes spent doing anything else. "When I was young, and a virgin, it seemed crazy to think that two people would have sex and then put their clothes on and go out in the world and be normal," Shane confides in me. "How can you do that? Isn't there something weird about that?" And yet, she notes, as an adult, "I don't walk around thinking to myself ever, *Oh, you've probably fucked*"—she pauses for a second, trying to think of an accurate, not overinflated number—*"three hundred and fifty people."*

Acknowledging that a woman has had sex with someone— or multiple someones—reveals far less about her, or the encounter, than we tend to think. Sex is an umbrella term that encompasses a wide array of experiences. Even if we limit ourselves to the strict, limited, heterosexist penis-in-vagina definition of erotic activity, there's still a number of different forms an encounter can take. If a woman notes that she's had sex with a man, is she saying that they had an intense emotional and physical connection that spanned several decades, or does she mean they had an unsatisfying bathroom quickie that lasted a few minutes and left her wanting? Was the sex something that permanently affected her, or was it a forgettable encounter whose details evaporated from her memory the minute it was over? Why are we convinced that even the briefest genital interaction leaves a man with a deep, intimate knowledge of a woman and a woman forever changed?[2]

A particularly noxious display of this belief can be found in many abstinence-only sex education curricula. In an attempt to demonstrate the supposed hazards of premarital sex, instructors will hold up a clean piece of tape, its pristine state representing the "purity" of a virginal woman. Over the course of the activity, the instructor attaches the piece of tape to the arms of several male students, with each adhesion serving as a metaphorical representation of sex. By the end of the demonstration, the tape is filthy and incapable

---

[2] A sentiment that is, of course, deeply embedded in our ideas about virginity as well.

of bonding to anyone's skin—and so too, the instructor suggests, is a woman who's had sex with multiple men.[3]

If you come from a more liberal background, it's easy to
see the dirty-tape demonstration as a backward and wrong-
headed product of conservative ideology. But even the most
liberal among us are frequently guilty of buying into similarly damaging ideas about what it means to have multiple
sex partners.

You've probably heard about the myth of the "loose vagina," for instance, which suggests that the more partners
a woman takes on, the more worn-out her vagina becomes,
eventually rendering it cavernous and presumably unplea-
surable to any but the most massive of members. There's
no truth to any of that: vaginal "tightness" is about muscle
strength and tension, not some inherent and limited elastic-
ity, and tighter vaginas aren't inherently more pleasurable
for anyone. But the myth is so ingrained that publications as
diverse as *Jezebel*, *Men's Health*, *Slate*, *Psychology Today*, and
LA Weekly have all devoted space to debunking it. Piece after
piece enlists doctors to remind readers that no, you can't tell
how many partners a woman's had just by inspecting her vagina, and no, there's not some number of sex partners that
will automatically render a woman's genitalia completely
unrecognizable from their original, virginal state—and yet
jokes about hot dogs and hallways nevertheless persist.

Equally hardy is the notion that having multiple partners makes a woman disease-ridden, as though STIs spon-
taneously generate after a woman's had a certain number

---

[3] There are a number of variations on this exercise: some involve a piece of chew-
ing gum, others a repeatedly used toothbrush. In some versions, two pieces of
tape are used to represent both the male and female partners in a couple, but
more often than not, the burden of purity is primarily placed on the woman.

of partners, regardless of whether she's using condoms or getting tested or taking any number of prophylactic precautions. In a scene from 2015's *Trainwreck*, love interest Aaron tells the lead, Amy, "It does bother me that you smoke pot and drink a lot and sleep with a lot of guys. It doesn't make me feel safe." What he means by "safe" is left open to interpretation, but it's not a stretch to assume he's trying to say that Amy's sexual history puts his own health at risk—a sentiment that's particularly baffling, given that the character is supposed to be a doctor and thus should be well aware that, regardless of Amy's sexual activity, he's perfectly capable of taking his sexual health and safety into his own hands.

Men who wield the STI argument as a defense of their disdain for sexually experienced women are demonstrating "a kind of primitive sense of how condoms work, as though they're magic," Shane tells me. "You know, condoms only work up until your fiftieth partner, and then they don't work anymore." It should go without saying that having more sexual partners does not automatically put you more at risk. When used properly, condoms work phenomenally well, and even unprotected sex only puts you at risk of contracting an STI if your partner already has one. You're far less likely to contract chlamydia from sex with one thousand uninfected partners than lifelong monogamy with someone with an untreated case of it.[4] The idea that sexually experienced women are inherently a health risk is more magical thinking than medical science, yet we still cling to the idea that it's grounded in reality, the same way abstinence-only

---

[4] Not that contracting chlamydia is something to be ashamed of, anyway: STIs are manageable, treatable, and far too stigmatized in our society.

educators offer up a piece of dirty tape as "proof" that sex is inherently harmful.

"It's just science that you shouldn't be a slut, it's not my hang-up," Shane quips, rolling her eyes as she recounts the many times that men have used nonsensical "health" concerns as a way to police her sexual behavior. The argument is rendered that much more ludicrous by the fact that the men most likely to profess fear of the risks posed by promiscuous women also seem to be the least likely to get tested, use condoms, or in any way take action to protect their sexual health. It's this hypocrisy, this insistence on positioning women as the vector of disease, that most angers Shane— and it's this inconsistency that leads me to believe that men who police women's sexual history in the name of sexual health and safety are masking a deeper insecurity.

"How do you define good sex?" Dan Savage asks me. Is it important to be the best sex a partner's ever had—and even if they swear up and down that it is, will you actually believe them? "On some level you're always going to worry that they're telling you the sex is great because they want other stuff from you," Savage continues. "And is that not enough? For that other stuff to be great enough that they're willing to settle for the sex that they have with you?"

It's a theme explored in Kevin Smith's *Chasing Amy*, a 1997 film about a comic book artist who falls for a lesbian only to learn that her sexual history is vastly more complicated than he'd thought.[5] In Smith's telling, the panic around women's pasts is rooted in a fear of not measuring up. While protagonist Holden is thoroughly comfortable with

---

[5] And, I should note, one of my favorite films.

his girlfriend Alyssa's extensive sexual experience when he's convinced he's her first male partner, learning that she's fucked many other men—often in creative and kinky ways— leaves him feeling unmoored. At the film's climax, Holden tells Alyssa that a threesome she had in high school puts them on uneven footing, The solution, he's decided, is for her to participate in a threesome with him and his room-mate, Banky. Once they've shared this experience, he's sure he'll be able to put her past behind him; it's the imbalance between their experience levels—and the fear that he can't live up to all the things she's done—that's made their rela-tionship rocky, he insists.

This logic—which, to its credit, *Chasing Amy* rejects— underpins so many of our discussions around female sexual experience. There's a deep-seated notion that having "the best" sex that a partner has ever had is a fundamental qual-ity of a lasting, healthy relationship. And the more people a woman has had sex with, the higher her standards presum-ably become with regard to sexual pleasure,[6] potentially rais-ing the bar for "good in bed" to impossibly high levels.

But the idea that balls-to-the-wall, mind-blowing, crazy sex is something all of us want from our partners is flawed to begin with. "Sometimes the best sex is nonrelationship sex. People go for it when they don't think they're ever going to see you again, and may not want to see you again," Savage tells me. Many of the things that make sex feel hot—a lack of inhibition, a sense of naughtiness and taboo, a willingness to show your kinkiest and most depraved side—can be easiest to access outside of the comfortable, committed structure of

---

[6] The irony here being that most sexually experienced heterosexual women will tell you that, if anything, their sexual adventures lowered the bar—mostly reveal-ing that, well, a lot of men are very bad at sex.

a relationship, and sometimes the people it's easy to access that side of ourselves with are people we'd never want to be in a relationship with in the first place. "Someone who outside of a relationship may just go for it...in a relationship that same person will be a lot more hesitant and tentative and self-conscious. Because the stakes are higher."

But even if sex within a relationship isn't, or can't be, as crazy as a one-night stand, or that vacation fling, or some other memorable evening, that doesn't mean it's not enjoyable, that we don't love it, or that it's not worth having. Trying to compare sexual experiences and sexual partners in the hopes of coming up with some definitive ranking of sexual compatibility is a futile exercise. Charlotte Shane—who, it should be noted, is now in a monogamous, committed relationship—offers this insight, as she tries to explain to me what, exactly, "good sex" means to her: "If you asked me to describe some really hot sex I remember, we could be here all day, surely, and there would be almost no commonality [between different experiences] except that it was all somehow what turned me on at the time. The guys would look really different; the circumstances would be really different; what exactly they did or said would be really different. But for some reason, all the stars were aligned for that to be crazy hot to me in that moment."

According to Hills, we're frequently taught to think of men as "authority figures" while women are "young people [who need] to be taught the ways of the world." And that may explain why, when men lie about their sexual histories, they tend to be more likely to exaggerate rather than minimize—to pad out their sexual résumés with experiences that suggest they're more knowledgeable, desirable, and capable of providing their partners with intense sexual pleasure than they actually are. Sexual experience is rarely thought to detract from a straight man's appeal; to the contrary, to many people it suggests that he's a worldly, attractive specimen who'll be able to confidently guide a woman to the highest peaks of pleasure.

But there is one type of sexual experience that men have a tendency to hide. "Men lie about same-sex experience, because women don't want to hear about it," Savage tells me. "Women find out their boyfriend saw a musical once and send me a panicked letter about how he might be gay. To find out your boyfriend sucked a dick once, or received a blow job once from a dude—[most women] have this never-ending panic attack about how he's secretly gay or must be gay," even in cases in which the women themselves have had same-sex experiences and still consider themselves straight.

As Savage speaks, I'm reminded of a phrase the writer Brian Moylan has bandied about, a theory he likes to call "the one dick rule." According to our collective understanding of sexuality, the penis is so powerful, so magical, that even the briefest exposure to it renders one forever changed. A man who's touched another penis is absolutely, definitely gay no matter how many women he's been with in his life; a woman who's been with one man is forever marked by him. There is, of course, an undercurrent of gay panic to this rule, but it's also indicative of how much sovereignty we afford to the penis. It's not just an oddly shaped sack of erectile tissue, flesh, and nerves; in our cultural imagination it is the absolute measure of one's sexual worth and identity, a thing that wields power equally over both men and women.

And yet despite all the hype, a penis is, well, just a penis. "The first time I sucked a dick I was like, 'Well, that was no big deal,'" Savage tells me. He'd been convinced, going in, that his fellatious act would incur the wrath of God, opening up the skies to reveal a puking deity, whose disgust would flood the streets with vomit. "And that didn't happen. It was like, 'Well that was just a dick in my mouth. I could do that again.'" Which, to be honest, is a pretty accurate description of most sexual experiences—in spite of the world-shattering, transformative power we still insist on ascribing to them.

"The bar is set higher for male-on-male intimacy for straight guys. The social consequences are more severe for men," Savage tells me. "To think, 'He couldn't have done that if he wasn't [gay],' there's a certain logic there. If he just was mildly curious, he probably wouldn't do it, because if people found out it would be potentially devastating. So why would he do that, except if he *had* to; he really really wanted to be- cause he's really gay. A woman can eat a little pussy, and no one says she's a lesbian. A woman can be a lesbian for four years and then say she's not, and no one's like, 'You're still secretly a lesbian.'"

Indeed, straight women are far more likely to play up same-sex experiences than hide them. There's the old trope of straight girls making out with one another or playing up some lightly sapphic experiences for male attention. But while straight women often benefit from a hint of sexual ex- perience with other women—and can shed their queer pasts with relative ease if they so choose—queer women who've had straight experiences aren't always given the same free- dom. Though Savage tells me that he never gets letters from lesbians fretting over how many pussies their partners have eaten, or worrying that they're too sexually experi- enced to find happiness with another woman, lesbians who date bisexual women display some of the same insecurities straight men do about their partners' past encounters with penises.

I initially reached out to Wendy C. Ortiz because I assumed her teenage sexual exploits—chronicled in the memoir *Excavation*—would have given her experience with the kind of shaming that leads women to obscure the details of their sexual pasts. But while Ortiz, who spent her early teens in a relationship with her middle school English teacher, certainly had her tales of being slut-shamed by men, she'd largely shrugged off that shame and insecurity by her early twenties. What was harder for her to push past, however, was a fear that—as a woman who'd spent the first three decades of her life predominantly in heterosexual relationships—she'd never quite be queer enough to gain acceptance from women who love women.

Ortiz began to understand herself as bisexual in her late teens, but finding a place within the LGBTQ community took significantly longer. As a student at Evergreen State College—a liberal arts college in Olympia, Washington, a town Ortiz tells me "has this reputation of being queer central"—she dreamed of coming out and finding community support and acceptance. But things didn't work out that way. According to Ortiz, "It felt almost as though among these folks, I still could not be completely myself. I could not have my sexual history just be out there. There were a few times where I had experiences where I know I was being judged for calling myself bisexual—there was definitely biphobia in that community."

The story Ortiz tells me is a familiar one, one that mirrors my own discomfort in some LGBTQ spaces. Despite rejecting the strictures of heteronormativity, certain corners of the LGBTQ community have simply set up a kind of parallel homonormativity, one where we are all "born this way," where "gold stars" are awarded to those who've entirely abstained from heterosexual contact, where you can only be straight *or* gay, and that determination is entirely based on the relationship you're presently in.

Ortiz isn't the only queer woman to feel boxed in by expectations and labels. Over the years, I've known countless women who've fretted that past or current attractions to men might somehow call their queer bona fides into question. One particularly prominent example of the policing of queer identity is actress Cynthia Nixon. Until her late thirties, Nixon exclusively dated men, including a fifteen-year relationship with Danny Mozes, with whom she'd had three children. After Nixon and Mozes split, she began dating Christine Marinoni (now her wife)—and found that gaining recognition and support from the LGBTQ community required more than just a serious relationship with a woman.

To many, Nixon's present gayness was rendered suspect by her past heterosexuality; acceptance as a woman-loving woman required a renunciation of her past as a woman who'd loved men. In an interview with the *New York Times* that ran in January 2012, Nixon notes that "people think I was walking around in a cloud and didn't realize I was gay, which I find really offensive. I find it offensive to me, but I also find it offensive to all the men I've been out with." Nixon wholeheartedly rejected the story line of a closeted youth and feigned heterosexual attractions, noting elsewhere that "I've been with men all my life and I'd never fallen in love with a woman. But when I did, it didn't seem so strange. I'm just a woman in love with another woman." That experience of sexual fluidity may explain why, in the same *Times* piece, Nixon is quoted as saying that "for me, [being gay] is a choice"—a line that set off its own kerfuffle as queer commentators argued that Nixon's "choice" rhetoric served only to give ammunition to antigay zealots hawking gay conversion therapy.

In a subsequent interview with the *Daily Beast*, Nixon is further pressed to clarify her sexual history and identity, as the interviewer asks, "Were you a lesbian in a heterosexual relationship? Or are you now a heterosexual in a lesbian relationship?" Nixon rejects this limited, binary setup, acknowledging that her identity is probably best understood as bisexual, but that—as a woman currently in love with another woman—she prefers to identify as gay, because "nobody likes the bisexuals." Nixon's coming-out experience, made that much clumsier by its incredibly public nature, revealed some uncomfortable truths about our ideas about sexual identity. Even in communities supposedly founded on the principles of sexual freedom, we're still expected to fit into a box, to have a predictable, simple-to-explain sexual history—and when that sexual history involves penises, queer women can be subjected to scrutiny just as strict as any straight woman.

"It's very difficult for people to accept that our identity changes," Ortiz tells me. "But for those of us whose identities change, and continue to change, and we acknowledge it, it's not that weird." Like Nixon, Ortiz has been in a committed relationship with another woman for years, and yet she still feels a twinge of anxiety whenever she's asked to present at a queer event. "In spaces that identify more as gay or lesbian [rather than queer], I still feel like I am the weird baby queer at forty-three years old who doesn't have the same kind of histories as the people that I'm sitting with," she tells me.

"And I start to wonder, if they knew my whole history, would they still accept me in this group?"

Although many women worry about being judged for whatever sex they've had, others fret instead about being judged for not having had sex at all. Despite our celebration of female purity, after a certain age, virginity becomes more of a burden than a bragging right, less a sign that you're a good girl than that you're somehow not good enough. In the public imagination, older virgins are either religious zealots, unattractive weirdos, or people for whom the act holds a particularly high value, and the longer one goes without experiencing sex, the bigger a deal that first sexual experience is presumed to be.

"There's a tipping point where after a certain age, if you are a virgin, then you have to lie about that and say that you're not," says Therese Shechter, director of the documentary *How to Lose Your Virginity*. In the Ask Trixie advice column she runs on the film's website, she's fielded a number of questions from women who—still virgins at twenty-five or thirty or older—worry that if someone they're interested in discovers they've never experienced sex, the other person will immediately lose interest. Women ask her if they should pretend to have had a partner or two, or go into the experience just neglecting to mention it happens to be their first time. Shechter understands exactly where they're coming from. A virgin until the age of twenty-three, she chose not to tell her first sexual partner about her total lack of experience—although in Shechter's case, the lie became quickly apparent, and she ended up owning up to her virginity.

Other women have more success obscuring their sexual innocence. When Lynn was thirty, she decided she wanted to experience sex for the first time and that, contrary to our standard story of first-time sex, she didn't want to make that big a deal of the whole thing. Because she worried that the man she'd picked for the experience—a twenty-six-year-old she'd been on a handful of dates with—wouldn't share her nonchalant attitude to first-time sex, she decided to keep him in the dark. That decision felt even more justified as he began to tell her about taking his twenty-three-year-old ex-girlfriend's virginity, something he clearly felt was a really big deal.

Despite existing at opposite ends of the sexual spectrum, older virgins and sexually experienced women feel compelled to lie for the exact same reason: they're told that there's a very narrow path to happiness and healthy relationships, and openly acknowledging you fall outside it can feel like an admission that you're somehow unworthy of your own happy ending.

That feeling of unworthiness can get even more intense when it's not merely your behavior but your entire attitude toward sex that's out of step with societal expectations. Annette, a thirty-four-year-old tech worker from Vancouver, is another older virgin I connected with—though unlike the situation of many other virgins, her lack of sexual experience isn't due to a lackluster dating life. To the contrary, Annette has been with her husband for well over a decade. The reason she hasn't had sex is that she's just never felt any kind of sexual attraction—or, as she puts it to me, "I don't get the itch."

When Annette first met her husband, she told him that she "didn't like to be touched," a not entirely accurate description of her lack of sexual desire. "I told him I didn't know how long, if ever, it would be until I'd want to have sex," she tells me over Skype. "I think he underestimated the truth of the statement. I think he assumed that it wouldn't be as bad."

Annette and her husband initially treated her lack of libido as a problem to be fixed, a sign that there was something wrong with her, or that she just hadn't discovered the specific key to unlocking her sexual side. And so she looked everywhere for a solution to this problem: she explored porn, she visited a wide range of medical professionals, she endured uncomfortable ultrasounds in the hopes that someone would uncover the key to her missing libido. And though a part of her remained unsure that she would ever be interested in sex, she allowed herself—and her husband—to believe that she'd be "normal" soon.

In the outside world, Annette grew increasingly tight-lipped about her sexless marriage. The few times she admitted that she didn't find sex compelling, she'd wound up bombarded with unsolicited advice, as friends insisted she couldn't possibly have an opinion on the matter if she'd never actually experienced it. "I've had someone actively want to be my sexual mentor," she tells me, noting that the advice to push past her comfort zone always felt like a way of saying, "Let me help you stop being you."

Eventually, Annette started hiding her lack of libido: when friends discussed their sex lives, she'd smile and nod, letting her silence imply that she knew exactly what they were talking about—that she, too, was having plenty of sex and totally fit in. Acknowledging her nonexistent sex life felt like admitting she was failing as a wife. Just as it was easier to keep telling her husband that eventually they'd be as sexually active as every other couple, it was simpler to let her friends think that her romantic life was exactly as raunchy as theirs.

And then, at thirty-three, Annette had a revelation. She wasn't broken. She didn't need to be fixed. She was asexual: a person who naturally lacks sexual feelings and attractions. Coming to terms with her sexual identity as a natural variation, rather than a disorder, was incredibly liberating. After years of feeling like someone who was failing to be a normal, sexually active adult, she now understood herself as just another kind of queer. And being able to identify as asexual—to put forth a more concrete identity than merely "I'm not interested in sex"—has enabled her to be more open and honest with her friends.

What's telling to me, even more than Annette's years of deception and dissembling around her lack of sexual desire, is the way that having a label offered her some degree of freedom from the judgments and shaming. So long as our desires (or lack thereof) follow one of a handful of pre-approved scripts, we're relatively free from judgment. It's when we venture off to create our own paths that things start to get messy. The problem is that for most of us, life rarely adheres to a script as simple as the one we're offered.

Halfway through our lunch, Charlotte Shane and I are still talking about men's complicated attitude toward safer sex and condoms—and the way so many men paradoxically combine a paranoid, near-irrational fear of STIs with a complete and total unwillingness to take any of the actions that might actually protect them.

"Men sometimes talk about [sexual health] like, 'Well, we'll just never know if you have an STI or not.' No, we will know.

The resistance I've encountered from straight men to getting tested for STIs is outrageous," Shane tells me. "There are men who will profess to feeling really anxious about their health, and yet they will not do this incredibly easy, basic thing." Their actions suggest that they firmly believe that sexual health is a woman's responsibility, an attitude Shane sums up as, "You're responsible for keeping me safe. I never want to even ask my doctor to give me a test. But all the women I'm fucking better be doing the right thing and not exposing me to danger."

STIs aren't the only sexual danger women are expected to protect men from. Unplanned pregnancy, too, is presented as something women do to men, poking holes in condoms and lying about contraceptive use in the hopes of "trapping" men with paternity. But the truth about who manipulates whom, and who needs to be afraid of being tricked into being a parent, is far more complicated than the stories we've been told.

CHAPTER SEVEN

I'm on the Pill

FEW OF US are eager to hear detailed accounts of how, exactly, our parents conceived us, but for my friend Denise, the subject is a particularly uncomfortable one. During an emotional fight a few years back, her mother began sobbing, tearfully acknowledging that she'd been a terrible mother. And then, in the midst of the drama, she dropped a bombshell: "I was conceived because she poked holes in a condom with a pin," Denise says.

As Denise understands the story, her mother—who would have been in her mid-twenties around this time—"wanted kids desperately," while her father was inclined to wait a few years. Denise's father had a career he was still trying to get off the ground; Denise's mother, on the other hand, didn't have a career to devote her energy to, and "she was desperate to start what she saw as her main thing in life." Sabotaging prophylactics felt like the only way to get what she wanted, and so sabotaging prophylactics became the way she began her family.

A few decades later, another young married woman was also misleading her partner about her contraceptive use—though in Karen's case, avoiding pregnancy, rather than achieving one, was the goal she had in mind. At twenty-one, Karen had married a man who was firmly against her being on birth control; as far as he was concerned, a woman who took birth control pills was a woman who planned to cheat on her partner. Deeply in love, and convinced that the rhythm method would protect her from pregnancy, Karen agreed to go off the pill. But mere months into their marriage, she learned the hard way that the rhythm method is only effective if you're incredibly rigorous about it. After giving birth at twenty-two, she began to have doubts about her husband's stance on birth control.

Though their sex life was fairly sporadic at this point, largely owing to her husband's abusive tendencies, there were still times when Karen felt affection and desire for her husband. And when he was inside of her, on the verge of orgasm, "What control did I really have besides saying, 'Please don't come inside me'?" she asks me. Even that limited option wasn't really available to her: "I didn't have that control, because that would have started another fight." Instead, she says, "I would go and buy Plan B," a huge ordeal that involved secretly purchasing the medication and taking it at work, all while being careful to dispose of any evidence to prevent her husband from discovering her secret. Karen eventually went back on the birth control pill, but the complication of having to hide it from her husband compromised her ability to consistently adhere to the pill's schedule. Three years after the birth of her first child, Karen wound up pregnant again.

Women like Denise's mother are whom we tend to think of when we hear that a woman is lying about birth control. But women like Karen should not be ignored. Pop culture suggests it's baby-hungry women who are sabotaging contraceptives: the tactic has popped up in a diverse range of movies and TV shows, including *Gone Girl, The Cosby Show, Degrassi: The Next Generation, Peep Show, Scrubs, Law & Order,* and virtually every soap opera ever produced. But studies have shown that men are much more likely to exert control over whether and how their partners get access to condoms, pills, and other essential tools for pregnancy and STI prevention. The American Congress of Obstetrics and Gynecology specifically defines reproductive coercion—the technical term for sabotaging birth control—as a "male behavior." Similarly, an overview of literature about reproductive coercion titled "Reproductive Coercion: Uncloaking an Imbalance of Social Power," which appeared in the January 2016 issue of the *American Journal of Obstetrics and Gynecology,* treats male victims as an also-ran, noting that "reproductive coercion involves behavior that interferes with contraceptive and pregnancy choices of women and occasionally men."

Birth control has long been lauded as a way for women to take control of their reproductive destinies. But sometimes, the pill is not enough. Sometimes, women need to turn to subversive tactics in order to truly gain autonomy over their bodies.

When I first began to explore the topic of women lying about sex, concealed ovulation—the fact that human bodies don't readily reveal when pregnancy is a possibility, creating an air of mystery around the timing of impregnation—seemed like an obvious explanation for our obsession with feminine deceit. In most mammals, ovulation is incredibly noticeable, accompanied by hard-to-ignore signs like swollen labia, spotting, and an actual interest in sex. In humans, on the other hand, ovulation is a bit more mysterious. While there are certainly physical signs associated with human ovulation—basal body temperature rises, cervical mucus changes consistency—they're not as readily apparent as a set of swollen red labia, particularly since, unlike some other mammals, humans are happy to get it on no matter where they might be in the ovulation cycle. Unless you're actively tracking your cycle, there's a good chance you won't know when you happen to be ovulating, and, by extension, neither will anyone you happen to be having sex with.

Because concealed ovulation is a relatively rare phenomenon among mammals, its existence within humans has sparked a good deal of discussion in the scientific community. There's no real consensus as to why humans evolved to have this particular quirk, and the theories that have been proposed vary widely. Some argue that concealed ovulation arose as a way for women to wield power over men, by making it harder to assess when someone has been impregnated and, of course, by whom; others have suggested that, to the contrary, concealed ovulation is a way for the reproductive imperative to wield its power over women (since if they knew when they could get pregnant, they'd be more likely to avoid it—as, of course, contraception has enabled women to do). But whatever the evolutionary basis for concealed ovulation, it's undeniable that it's had an impact on the way that men view—and treat—women. Concealed ovulation shrouds conception—and, by extension, women's bodies themselves—in mystery, denying men full access to the entirety of the female experience. In response, men have furtively, and often futilely, devoted themselves to decoding women's bodies, couching the mysteries of women's lived experience in myth, and using this lack of transparency as an excuse to track and control women, to monitor their behavior and limit their comings and goings,[1] and, at times, to even erase women entirely.

"Many of us live as fictions.... Women's bodies are fictions to the men who describe them and determine our reproductive capacities," Aliza Shvarts, an artist and teaching fellow at the Whitney Museum, tells me. As an undergraduate at Yale University, Shvarts developed a performance art project that—perhaps unsurprisingly, given its content—ultimately incited an international media frenzy. The untitled art project, conceived as Shvarts's senior thesis, was intended to examine questions about the nature of reproduction and women's awareness of, and autonomy over, the workings of their own bodies. For the length of the project, Shvarts spent the days surrounding her ovulation self-inseminating with donated semen; on the twenty-eighth day of her cycle, she would take an herbal abortifacient, inducing bleeding that could be read as either an early-stage miscarriage or just a body that had never been pregnant in the first place shedding its menstrual lining as per usual (the inherent unknowability here was an essential part of Shvarts's piece).

But the questions Shvarts originally sought to explore were ultimately subsumed once her project caught the eye of the media. As detractors deemed the work "gruesome and pornographic," deriding Shvarts herself as "insensitive" and, in the words of Wanda Franz, the president of the National Right to Life Committee, "a serial killer," the Yale administration sought to distance itself from the controversy, banning Shvarts from displaying the video and final installation,

---

[1] It's reasonable to assume that the entire virginity obsession is at least partly due to concealed ovulation: if it were easy to assess when someone was ovulating, it'd be relatively simple to track the paternity of someone's offspring, rendering "purity" far less important when it comes to tracking who fathered whose child.

and—in a somewhat fitting end—deeming the work a "creative fiction," rather than a documentation of Shvarts's lived truth and bodily experience.

To Shvarts, the controversy surrounding her work was not merely a debate about what is and is not suitable art for a student to produce at Yale, but of a piece with a long history of the policing and control of women's bodies, sexuality, and place within reproduction. On a very basic level, the form of Shvarts's art piece wasn't much different from the routine Plan B[2] use that Karen engaged in during her marriage. But while Karen furtively hid her contraceptive use and quest for bodily autonomy, Shvarts conducted her process out in the open, violating social norms about how women are supposed to view their reproductive potential. In the process, Shvarts attracted hordes of commentators who felt qualified to weigh in on what, exactly, she had a right to do with her body and in what fashion, echoing the debates over women's reproductive rights that have been going on for years.

Though much of the discussion of Shvarts's piece has centered on what was present—Yale administrators, she notes, were particularly fixated on what, exactly, she'd done with her vagina and where, exactly, semen had been involved—it's equally worth considering the one thing that was absent. For all the fixation on semen and insemination, men do not factor into the project at all, mentioned only as "fabricators" who donated material to be used in Shvarts's art. Shvarts notes that she's baffled by "the idea that men even feel they should be centered in reproduction." Throughout history, men have sought to diminish the role that women play in the work performed by their own bodies, reducing women

---

[2] Plan B is not an abortifacient, of course.

to vessels, to incubators, merely here to sustain and feed and support the life of which men have routinely portrayed themselves as the sole authors and creators.[3] And it's that sense of ownership of the reproductive process that likely leads men to insert themselves into the very personal decisions women make about the state and status of their bodies, that leads many men to take aggressive, and sometimes deceptive, action to maintain control of whether, how, and when women do and do not get pregnant.

"A lot of people aren't super familiar with reproductive coercion," Bianca Palmisano tells me. Even among physicians, experiences like Karen's aren't automatically seen as anything out of the ordinary. But men who try to control their partners' reproductive choices aren't just bad boyfriends, or guys doing their best to gain a little control over their own reproductive future. They're abusers, ones whom women often have to go to complicated, and sometimes deceptive, lengths to protect themselves from. That's something Palmisano, a sex educator and medical consultant who trains physicians to recognize the signs of sexual violence, is doing her best to raise awareness about.

One of the problems Palmisano—and anyone who works in the abuse prevention space—has to combat is that most of us don't really know what an abusive relationship actually looks like. Media depictions of relationship abuse tend to play up the physical violence aspect. Bruises, black eyes, and broken wrists are treated as the be-all and end-all of relationship abuse; in actuality, physical violence is just one

---

[3] The notion of the homunculus—a fully realized, miniature human that a man ejaculates into a woman's womb, where it grows into a full-sized offspring—is a very literal depiction of this idea.

manifestation of a toxic relationship, not the sum total of the toxicity itself.

While physical abuse is a component of many toxic relationships—and violence itself a strong indicator of the existence of abuse—it's best thought of as a dangerous tool that abusers wield to achieve their ultimate goal. Most abusers don't hit their partners solely for the thrill of physical violence. Instead, physical intimidation is a way of keeping a partner submissive, in line, and under one's control. And as a result, it's just one of many tools that abusers can turn to. But there are other, often less visible, tactics that abusers use to wield control over their partners.

Of these tactics—which can include humiliating and belittling a partner, exerting total control over their finances, or even using the legal system to harass them through repeated lawsuits—reproductive coercion is a particularly effective one. As Karen discovered firsthand, once someone has impregnated you, it's significantly harder to end the relationship. Even if you walk out on your partner, you're still permanently bonded to them through your shared offspring—offspring your abuser may legally have a right to spend time with.

For many abuse victims, leaving isn't—or doesn't feel like—an option. Victims routinely stay with their abusers out of an often very justified fear that leaving will result in pain and suffering far worse than they're currently experiencing. Depending on one's situation, separating from your abuser can mean losing access to your children or other family members, suffering shame and stigma within your community, being subjected to online harassment and public humiliation, and, in the most extreme cases, even death.

Even without explicit threats of violence or retaliation, abuse victims often stay in their relationships for the same reason that any of us stay in relationships we know aren't very good for us. "We've all been in relationships that probably weren't very good for us: we weren't well matched, maybe we fought a lot, or there just was something that wasn't working. But the reason that we were involved in them was because we saw something good," Palmisano tells me. "At the end of the day you love that person, and so you want to try to make it work. And there's no definitive line in the sand when you're inside of that relationship that says, 'Okay, this has gone too far.' Everything feels like it has a lot of nuance to it because it's within the container of that relationship that you care about. I think there are a lot of people who stay in relationships that aren't very good for them because of that emotional connection." And in a society that puts a great deal of pressure on us to partner up and stay that way, "making it work" even in the face of abuse can sometimes feel like a moral imperative.

For those who find themselves in this position—unwilling or unable to leave a relationship, eager to avoid pregnancy but afraid to openly use contraception—deception can feel like the only way to retain control. And for the providers Palmisano works with, offering patients access to discreet forms of contraception can ultimately be thought of as a form of harm reduction. While getting a patient out of an abusive situation should always be a physician's ultimate goal, offering access to contraceptives that enable them to reclaim a bit of bodily autonomy can be an important first step.

Conveniently, the contraceptives best suited for someone evading a controlling partner are also the ones doctors are already eager to recommend to many of their patients, largely because the factors that make them appealing to an abuse victim also happen to make them extremely effective in the population at large. Long-acting, reversible contraceptives (commonly referred to as LARCs) like the IUD and Implanon, a hormonal implant, can take effect upon insertion and provide protection against pregnancy for anywhere from three to twelve years, meaning that a single doctor's appointment can potentially provide over a decade of highly effective contraception. With a LARC, there's no need to worry that a forgotten pill or sabotaging partner will lead to an unwanted pregnancy. Once they're in, they're in, with an effectiveness rate that exceeds 99 percent.

For abuse victims in particular, these methods have an added benefit. Though it can be hard to hide a pill pack or contraceptive ring from someone you're intimate with, implants and IUDs are, in most cases,[4] nearly undetectable, offering the ability to control your own fertility while letting a partner believe they're the ones who have final say over the matter.

And even for those who aren't in an abusive relationship— or any relationship at all—the discreet nature of most birth control methods can have an off-label benefit when it comes to navigating sex with men.

In the spring of 2017, a new term began popping up in media outlets: stealthing.

A slang term for the practice of removing a condom during sex without the knowledge or consent of one's partner,

---

[4] Although not in all cases. There are reports of partners detecting the IUD strings that protrude from the cervix; anecdotally, I've heard of at least one instance where a man discovered his partner's IUD strings and pulled on them to remove her IUD without her knowledge or consent.

stealthing—often referred to as a "disturbing new sex trend"—first began appearing in women's media like *Teen Vogue* but eventually found its way to a more widespread audience, with name checks in mainstream news publications like *USA Today*, the *New York Post*, and *Forbes*. The initial source of all this interest? A paper published in the *Columbia Journal of Gender and Law* titled "'Rape-Adjacent': Imagining Legal Responses to Nonconsensual Condom Removal."

Penned by Alexandra Brodsky, a feminist attorney and cofounder of Know Your IX, an organization that empowers students to end rape and abuse in their schools, the article is tonally quite different from the salacious sexual "trendspotting" articles it ultimately inspired. Brodsky does not suggest that nonconsensual condom removal[5] is new or necessarily on the rise. Rather, her goal is to acknowledge that it's problematic that it exists and that, troublingly, it is not recognized with a specific name or even officially considered a form of sexual assault. As Brodsky writes, "[victims] say they do not know what to call the harm and United States courts have not had occasion to address and name the practice"—a state of affairs that renders those who've experienced nonconsensual condom removal unsure how to categorize or discuss their trauma and incapable of seeking any form of legal recourse. As a first step toward remedying the harm suffered by these assault survivors, Brodsky's paper seeks not only to name and identify the problem but to offer proposed courses of legal action, exploring an array of options that might be made available to those who have experienced this harm.

---

[5] Brodsky actively dislikes the term "stealthing," noting that appending a cutesy term to an act of sexual violence trivializes it and minimizes the harm it causes.

When I reach out to Brodsky to discuss her findings, she is unequivocal about the motivations that lie behind non-consensual condom removal. Citing the work of Kelly Cue Davis, Brodsky tells me that "the likelihood that a man [will] sabotage a condom is directly correlated to his feelings about women,"[6] or, to put it more bluntly, "men who sabotage condom use or are deeply invested in convincing their partner[7] not to use a condom are misogynists."

It's an observation that's been backed up by Brodsky's own research as well. In writing her paper, Brodsky did not merely examine the harm experienced by the survivors of nonconsensual condom removal. She also spent a great deal of time reading through online message boards where men exchange tips on how to secretly remove condoms during sex—and, in the process, offer rationalizations for their abusive behavior. "Their justifications were rooted in male supremacy; in the idea that they had the right to spread their seed, that they had the right to do whatever they wanted with their partner's body." Brodsky's paper catalogues many of these justifications, quoting internet commenters who—in varied and colorful ways—argue that a woman who consents to sex automatically consents to sex without a condom, that it's both a man's right and his fundamental nature to ejaculate inside of a partner who consents to sex in any conceivable way.

---

[6] Davis's paper, "Young Men's Condom Use Resistance Tactics: A Latent Profile Analysis," published in the *Journal of Sex Research*, states that "stronger endorsement of negative attitudes towards women (including rape myth acceptance and hostility towards women) directly predicted greater engagement in coercive condom use resistance."

[7] Male *or* female partner, as nonconsensual condom removal also occurs during same-sex encounters.

And yet, even as proponents of nonconsensual condom removal advocate a variety of deceptive strategies for achieving their goal, "it was never portrayed as lying," Brodsky tells me. "Lying is a lady problem. [Removing a condom secretly] was about mastery, about being good at getting away with this, about mastering your partner"[8]—about successfully demonstrating male dominance in a heterosexual encounter.

Brodsky's paper went viral for a number of reasons. It gave the media a scary new sex "trend" to wring their hands over, offering fodder for both those itching to advocate for sexual assault survivors and those eager to stoke further panic about the dangers of casual sex (or, potentially, sex itself). And it also gave women a way to describe a previously nameless form of abuse—as well as a way to discuss related behavior that, while not quite stealthing, seems to stem from a similar belief that men are the ones who set the parameters during heterosexual sex.

"I once knew a guy who told me that he didn't like to ask his partners if they wanted to have sex because part of his skill as a sexual partner was 'knowing when they wanted it,'" Brodsky says. "He would basically penetrate them without conversation, which also precluded using condoms. It was just baffling to me that...he truly believed that that was what he was supposed to be doing as a male partner to women." For her, there's a clear link between this behavior and that of avowed stealthers: both stem from a place of sexism and misogyny, and to the extent that they differ, it's only by degree.

---

[8] A dichotomy that, Brodsky notes, resembles the way many of Donald Trump's deceits are discussed as him getting one over on the system, while women like Hillary Clinton are simply branded as fundamentally dishonest.

Tellingly, Davis's work treats deception as merely one of several ways that men engage in the behavior she terms "condom use resistance." Other strategies young men employ to coerce or manipulate partners into condom-free sex include withholding sex, emotionally manipulating a partner through guilt or professions of love, raising a partner's arousal level until they cease to resist, or even just insisting that condom-free sex bears no risk (a strategy that may be employed in combination with one or several others). While premeditated deception may be the most noxious and extreme sort of condom avoidance, focusing on stealthing to the exclusion of less extreme forms of coercion means ignoring the full range of abuses women experience at the hands of partners who feel entitled to condom-free sex.

To the best of my knowledge, I've never been stealthed. But I am intimately familiar with several of the other strategies detailed in Davis's research. Straight men who largely refuse to use condoms, even with casual sex partners, are a surprisingly common breed, and I found myself nodding in recognition as I read through the condom avoidance strategies detailed in her discussions with study participants. The condom avoiders in Davis's focus groups talk about downplaying the risks of condomless sex, upping a partner's arousal in the hopes of lowering her resistance, and guilting partners by arguing that condoms imply a lack of trust— all tactics and lines eerily similar to things I've witnessed firsthand.

Davis's research is primarily focused on the mindset of men who aggressively avoid condom use, but it's also worth discussing the impact this sort of behavior has on women, particularly with regard to how it shapes their interactions with men. From the time they hit puberty—and often long before that point—women are taught to think of themselves as sexual gatekeepers. They're taught to just say no, to clearly state their needs, to kick out any man who refuses to accept their terms. And as a result, they're taught to think that any sexual encounter that might go awry is a sign that they didn't gate-keep hard enough—that the men who might violate their trust and ignore their requests for condom use are just dudes being dudes, but the women who let them get away with it are shameful failures.

Reading through Brodsky's and Davis's work, it's clear that men who actively seek to avoid using condoms know exactly what they're doing. They know their partners are interested in using condoms, they know that they don't want to comply, and they're happy to employ whatever strategies they need—manipulation, deception, or potentially even physical force—to win over their partners or at least get their way. And yet in the aftermath, it's frequently women who are made to feel at fault for succumbing to a targeted campaign of persuasion, rather than men who are held accountable for violating the wishes of a partner.

When women[9] come forward about their experiences with nonconsensual condom removal, they're frequently told that they shouldn't have had sex with someone they couldn't trust, that they were at fault for bedding down with a dude before aggressively vetting him and confirming that he was truly "one of the good ones." But the reality is that it can be nearly impossible to ascertain whether someone is "truly" trustworthy until they've proven themselves otherwise. And for women who want to partake in casual sex—but don't want to deal with the hassle of being pressured into not using a

---

[9] Or, as a message board conversation that Brodsky highlights notes, gay men.

condom or potentially being stealthed—combatting a deceptive, manipulative condom avoider with a bit of one's own
deception can feel like evening the playing field. Especially
when the goal of that deception is purely to protect oneself
from the risks of condom-free sex.

According to Alyssa, a twenty-two-year-old who's based in
Brooklyn, casual hookups frequently unfold in a very specific way. She'll tell a potential sex partner that she wants
to use a condom, he'll respond by noting he'd assumed she
was on the pill. "If my answer is yes, the debate of 'Oh I'll
pull out, you're on the pill, it'll be fine' starts," she says.
It's a debate that rarely ends with pleasant, enjoyable sex.
Pointing out that condoms are the only effective way of
preventing STI transmission isn't met with an understanding nod—instead, the men Alyssa's had this conversation
with are more likely to assume that bringing STIs into the
conversation means she thinks they're dirty, diseased, and
untrustworthy.[10]

Rather than submit herself to an extended debate over
whether a condom is actually necessary, Alyssa cuts the
conversation off at the pass by telling her hookups that,
while she's technically on the pill, she keeps forgetting to
take it and thus can't be sure it's actually working. Once
she's done that, the fight over condom use is cut short—
partly because, despite their aversion to condoms, most of
her partners don't actually want to risk getting her pregnant[11]
and partly, Alyssa suspects, because presenting herself as a

---

[10] Which, to be honest, is a fairly reasonable assumption to make about a man
who tries to persuade someone he's only just met to eschew condoms, but I
digress.

[11] Among the men Alyssa hooks up with, pregnancy seems to be a bigger concern
than STIs, though this attitude is not universal.

dumb, forgetful girl makes her partners feel dominant and in charge.

For Alyssa, the tactic is akin to strategy she employs in her work as a portrait photographer. If a client seems uneasy in front of the camera, she tells me, "I'll say, 'Hold on, my settings are weird. I have to fix this,' and then I fiddle aimlessly with my camera. Without a doubt, they get more comfortable." Alyssa suspects that her feigned incompetence allows her clients to feel superior and relax in front of the camera—and while she doesn't enjoy pretending to be an idiot, "it results in better photos." Similarly, "forgetting" to take her pills isn't her ideal situation—she notes that the one time a man agreed to use a condom straightaway, with no pushback, the sex was much better for her—but it's preferable to a night of being badgered into unprotected sex.[12]

Though it may seem cold for Alyssa to position sex in these terms—treating the exchange as a power play, a situation that invites and requires Machiavellian manipulation—her attitude is largely a response to the way men frame sex in the first place. The men in Davis's study show little remorse when it comes to manipulating women or quickly discard those who push back and insist on using protection. One participant's explanation of the benefits of dating younger, or less experienced, women unintentionally turns into a celebration of gaslighting, as he explains to a moderator that "you're with a girl, and you're often times, she'll say something, and you point out everything that she says as kind of silly or wrong, and that's kind of like—I know guys that do that. And it's not like a bad thing, but it's like you're

---

[12] Particularly since, the one time she *did* give in to a request for condom-free sex, she ended up contracting an STI.

actually teaching the girl something. You're like challenging them. And if they have some silly idea about using a condom and you challenge them on that, too, and as a bonus, you get skin play, it's kind of cool." When men openly admit to going to these extensive lengths just to avoid using a condom, it's hard to feel pity when they're the victims of deceit in return.

When I ask Alyssa why she opts to have sex with men who are, by her own admission, "trash," she offers up a rationale that's familiar to anyone who's engaged in casual sex. "I'm not dating these men," she tells me. "When I'm seriously interested in a person, I'm going to take this seriously. And when that happens, I don't use these stupid tactics. I don't let bullshit slide. But these are just weekend things." For women who are interested in casual sex—and sometimes even women in committed relationships—safety and honesty can often feel mutually exclusive. If you can ensure the former by letting the latter slide, and still have the no-strings-attached fun you wanted in the first place, a little bit of lying doesn't feel like that high a price to pay. After all, Alyssa tells me, "most times they agree [to use a condom] in the end, after I pull these stupid tricks."

If women who hide their birth control—whether to evade nonconsensual impregnation or encourage condom use—are trying to reclaim a bit of bodily autonomy, what's to be made of women who do the reverse, secretly abandoning birth control in the hopes of getting pregnant? What motivates women to say, "I'm on the pill," when pregnancy prevention is the furthest thing from their minds?

During the audience discussion segment of an episode of *The Wendy Williams Show* from April 2014, host Williams chats with an audience member named Kendra who's considering abandoning her contraceptives without telling her husband. "I've been married for six years, and me and my husband just had our first baby girl about nine months ago," Kendra tells Williams. "Before we were married, he promised me that we would have two kids, and now he doesn't want any more. My friends think I should trick him and stop taking my birth control."

Williams, who tells Kendra that she doesn't like to encourage spousal lying, immediately backtracks on this policy and encourages Kendra to take her friends' advice. "Clap if you think that he should trick him," she instructs her audience, who respond with thunderous applause. As an explanation for her out-of-character endorsement of deceit, Williams tells Kendra that "men have never been in control of our bodies. We're the ones who are in control." It's a declaration that's baffling, as the amount of energy that women have devoted to the reproductive rights movement makes fairly clear that women don't feel in control of their bodies. And yet it's also telling: in Williams's eyes, it's not Kendra's husband whom Kendra seeks to gain control over, but rather her own body and reproductive destiny.

There is far less research on the number of women who attempt to "baby trap" their partners than there is on their male counterparts. While the *American Journal of Obstetrics and Gynecology* paper "Reproductive Coercion: Uncloaking an Imbalance of Social Power" cites a number of studies that profile women who experience reproductive coercion, with estimated rates as high as 25 percent depending on the population surveyed, only one cited source—the CDC's 2010 National Intimate Partner and Sexual Violence Survey—delves into the topic of men, estimating that 10.4 percent of men have had a partner who attempted to get pregnant against the man's will.[13]

The authors of the article see this paucity of data as a sign that more research needs to be done into the impact of reproductive coercion on men and, in particular, into the motivations of women who choose to manipulate their partners into impregnating them. And research would be useful because in its absence we're left mostly with pop culture representations of the phenomenon—ones that are, more often than not, created and promoted by men—and as a result, don't look too favorably on women.

The typical take on this lie goes something like this: Boy meets girl. Girl wants a commitment. Boy hesitates. Girl "accidentally" winds up pregnant—and boy is now tied to her for life. Whether it's out of love, desperation, or general insanity, women who fake their contraceptive use are presumed to be doing it for a man, one who'd all too happily cut ties if there weren't a baby in the picture. For men's rights activists, it's a sign that women are the ones who are truly in control, able to curtail a man's future by tricking him into impregnation. But are women truly "accidentally" getting pregnant in the hopes of solidifying a relationship?

It's certainly possible that some are, but the idea that a significant number of women are betting on a surprise pregnancy to lock in a relationship seems iffy. Having a child

---

[13] The CDC survey estimates that 8.6 percent of women have experienced reproductive coercion, a data point that some men's rights activists point to as proof that men are the real victims of reproductive coercion. But this claim seems dubious. A number of other studies have reported women experiencing reproductive coercion at significantly higher rates, and, tellingly, even the CDC survey results noted that women were 1.7 times as likely to report a partner refusing to use a condom. Further, comparing being forcibly impregnated to being nonconsensually placed on the hook for child support is a bit of a false equivalency.

is no guarantee of a committed relationship or even child support (as millions of single mothers across America can attest), and there are plenty of easier ways of securing financial stability than pregnancy and childbirth.

What seems more likely is that women who do lie about their birth control are women like Kendra, women who simply want to have children regardless of what their partners want. And while it may seem odd to frame a "surprise" pregnancy as a declaration of bodily autonomy, as Williams does, it makes a lot more sense that women who abandon birth control do so in an attempt to regain control of their own bodies, rather than in an attempt to take control of the lives of men.

When a woman sabotages her own birth control, or lies about being on it to begin with, the truth will eventually out: the pregnant body reveals the lie, making the deception palpable, even if not 100 percent provable. But when a woman successfully does the reverse, hiding her contraception in an attempt to avoid pregnancy or encourage condom use, the lie is more likely to stay hidden. Absence of pregnancy isn't firm proof of contraceptive use. For most women—even those who aren't on birth control—it's just the body's natural state of being.

And perhaps it's that imbalance between the lie that naturally reveals itself and the one that successfully stays hidden that fuels our cultural conviction that women, and not men, are the ones who initiate the manipulation, the ones who have the upper hand in the exchange. It's far harder to prove that women are lying to evade pregnancy rather than the reverse; for many, that lack of concrete proof serves as evidence that it probably isn't happening. Though Brodsky notes that the vast majority of responses she's received to her paper on nonconsensual condom removal have been people affirming the truth of her findings, "a quarter of the feedback I've gotten online has been, 'But what about women who lie about birth control?'" No matter how much evidence there may be of the harms routinely wrought by men, she says, "We can't have a conversation about contraceptive sabotage without falling back on this myth that it's a problem perpetuated by women."

There's another factor that helps to obscure the reality of who's manipulating whom. Unlike fake orgasms and makeup and our "numbers," women don't talk about hiding their birth control. They certainly don't talk about it with men, but they also rarely talk about it with other women. The rationale for the former is obvious: if hiding one's birth control use is going to be an effective strategy for self-protection, it's better if the person you're protecting yourself from remains ignorant that it's even a possibility. Women don't tell men about the lengths that they go to protect themselves out of a fear that doing so will make it even harder to stay safe.

It's a little more difficult to assess why women are relatively close-lipped around other women. But if I had to wager a guess, I'd say it's due to a sense of shame. Admitting you're hiding your birth control from a man you've opted to fuck means acknowledging that—in spite of the pervasive messaging that good girls make smart choices, that they only give their "precious gift" to men who deserve it, that they withhold sex from men who don't respect them—you're actively doing the opposite. It means admitting that your sex life is more important than your sense of safety or perhaps even self-respect, or that—worse still—you've managed to wind up in love with an abuser. Women who open up about taking this route risk being labeled slutty, stupid, foolish, or weak, rendering open dialogue about this behavior a wholly unappealing option.

Yet while women are incentivized to stay silent about their attempts at self-protection, men are likely to do just the opposite. Men who openly chat about women who "trap" men with their birth control lies aren't labeled weak-willed, foolish, or slutty—if anything, they're deemed magnanimous for attempting to warn other men who risk getting tied down. And that imbalance, that gendered disparity in who has the freedom to speak openly about safety and sex, has helped enshrine an inaccurate notion of who's truly at risk of having a partner sabotage their reproductive autonomy. We're so convinced that women, and not men, are the ones who are in control here that the actual truth is off-putting, and often offensive, to some. Brodsky saw this firsthand in the response to her findings on nonconsensual condom removal. The idea of men, and not women, being the perpetrators of contraceptive sabotage "was so counter to the narrative that is publicly available...that people couldn't wrap their heads around the idea that actually men could be the center of the story."

And it's not just internet commenters and angry men who are reinforcing this view of how the world works. During our conversation, Palmisano tells me about an exchange she had at a Baltimore conference for HIV educators. Palmisano was at the conference to educate attendees on how to collect information about a patient's sexual history in a positive, affirming, and comfortable way; as part of this process, she always invites the audience to consider all the negative, harmful messages they've received about sex over the course of their lives[14]—and, in many cases, still hold on to and repeat to patients, colleagues, and family members.

Over the years, Palmisano has heard many toxic messages, but the one that really stuck with her came from a mother in her fifties. As Palmisano relates the encounter to me, "[she] said, 'I always tell my son, "Make sure you date a girl for nine months before you have sex with her, because that way you'll know if she was pregnant when you met her."' This narrative that a woman might be lying about being pregnant so she could trap you in a relationship—[that] she just parroted that out without any shame or any reflection on what that meant actually about women was really startling to me. It's remarkable how much of that we're still dealing with, even with professionals who are supposed to be very sex positive."

It troubles Palmisano that even some of her colleagues in the sexual health space don't find messages like this to be problematic—but perhaps it shouldn't be surprising. It's not wrong to believe that women will lie to their sex partners if it gets them some kind of advantage; the mistake here is misunderstanding what sort of advantage motivates most women to lie. The pregnancy that will allegedly "trap" a man might seem like solid motivation to some, but for many more women, it's a desire to avoid pregnancy, to retain bodily autonomy, to enjoy sex on their own terms, free from the manipulations of men.

It's a subtle distinction, yet it's an incredibly important one. Because when all we know is that women lie—without

---

[14] An activity that, she tells me, "yields very interesting but frequently depressing results."

care or consideration for the context or motivation for that deceit—it becomes easy to believe that women lie about everything, with or without cause. It becomes easy to believe that women, and not men, are the ones most likely to instigate manipulation, to use deception to wield control over their relatively helpless partners.

It becomes easy to miss that most women lie because men don't listen to, or respect, their actual truths. And it becomes significantly harder to believe the words of the women who need our trust the most.

The language used to defend nonconsensual condom removal on "stealthing" boards can be stomach-turning in its naked misogyny. Women are discussed in callous, anatomical terms, their ability to advocate for their desires, needs, and physical and emotional safety outright dismissed in favor of what's "natural" (unprotected sex and internal ejaculation) and therefore what men have an unquestioned "right" to. The full-throated contempt for the idea that women are people, not body parts, that sex is a collaboration, not something that men take and women give up, is difficult to miss. But it is a mistake to assume that this mindset exists only among men who actively avoid using condoms with their partners.

The underlying sentiment that upholds the argument for nonconsensual condom removal—that women are passive recipients of sexual attention and men the ones who set the agenda for what unfolds during an erotic encounter—isn't unique to men who brag about manipulating their partners into unprotected sex. To the contrary, that notion is integral to many of our ideas about how sex between men and women is "supposed" to function, as well as the roles that men and women are taught to play in both sexual and romantic relationships. It pervades our pop culture, our pornography, and even our legislation. In North Carolina, a woman's ability to withdraw consent during sex still isn't legally recognized. Thanks to a 1979 North Carolina Supreme Court ruling, once a woman says yes to penetration, she's considered to have given the all clear. Even if her partner subsequently becomes violent, even if she begs him to stop, the experience is still considered consensual. Despite numerous attempts to overturn the statute, it still remains on the books.

"Men get to set the objective terms" of what sex and consent look like, Brodsky tells me. "What that really means is that if [a woman] consents to sex, she consents to all the sex that [a man] wants to have." When men are raised to believe that sex unfolds on their terms, and their terms alone, when women go through life deceiving and dissembling as a way to protect themselves from men's expectations, desires, and even their laws, it can be difficult for heterosexual sex to truly feel like an activity that's mutually enjoyed by two equal parties.

Even after decades of feminist advocacy, men are still the ones in charge, and women are still second-class citizens. Given the reality of that entrenched power imbalance, it seems worth asking: What exactly do we mean when we talk about consent?

CHAPTER EIGHT

No

ANDREA BARRICA WAS raised to think of sex as a transactional arrangement. The rules of the exchange were simple—"Men take it; women give it," Barrica explains—but the consequences were not. Sex wasn't just sex; it was power. And every time a woman acquiesced to a man's sexual interest, a bit of her power was chipped away. As her Catholic Filipino father bluntly explained, "No one likes easy girls—you have to play hard to get."

While her male cousins were given the freedom to pursue women and explore sex, Barrica's dating life was subjected to rigorous scrutiny. Her sexuality was treated as a public good. "My entire family was involved in decisions about whether I should be allowed to date," Barrica says; she was routinely humiliated in her family's endeavors to maintain and protect her virtue.

And she was also taught to lie. "We're told as women to play this game, where even if you want something, you have to actively pretend [you don't want it] and resist," Barrica tells me. To be open about one's sexual desire can come with a social cost, whether that's being shunned by society, shamed by your family, or treated as "damaged goods" by current or even future partners. A woman who wants to remain in good standing with her family, her culture, and her

---

community learns to emphasize her chastity at the expense of her libido. You say no even when you want to say yes. You reject sex until it's acceptable to consent.

The world that Barrica describes to me is one that's both incredibly foreign and intimately familiar. In our post–*Sex and the City* landscape, where *50 Shades of Grey* is a best-selling book and vibrators are sold at the drugstore, the idea that women can't be open and honest about their sexual desires feels like a dated one. Kate Harding, author of *Asking for It: The Alarming Rise of Rape Culture—and What We Can Do About It*, sees playing hard to get as something more out of her mother's generation than her own, and for women who were raised with feminist ideals, the idea that women lose status by saying yes to sex can seem laughable.

Yet the notion of seduction as a power exchange, one in which men pursue and women withhold, doesn't feel so far from the realities of modern sex. According to online dating site OkCupid, straight men are 3.5 times more likely to send the first message than straight women,[1] an expectation of men taking the lead that continues into the bedroom and extends all the way to the altar, with woman-initiated proposals still rare enough to merit a *New York Times* trend piece in 2016. Women may feel more comfortable saying yes to sex, but they still rely on men to initiate and set the tone for many of their encounters. And women are still relying on men to protect their health: a 2016 study by the Center for Sexual Health Promotion at Indiana University found that only 18 percent of women had purchased condoms for their

---

[1] The fact that competitor Bumble requires women to message first is novel enough to garner the site accolades, press, and the label "feminist."

last sexual encounter, while a full 65 percent had never purchased condoms at all.

Modern women may grow up surrounded by images of
sexually liberated women, but there's a disconnect between
what they're told is possible and the paths they're provided
to actually achieve it. Women have more sexual freedom
than ever, yet many still run up against the limits established by age-old ideas of female propriety. Even as we grow
up learning that yes means yes and no means no, men are
still learning to doubt women's demurrals, to treat their nos
as maybes, as opportunities for persuasion rather than full
stops. Even as women are raised to believe that the quality
of their sexual experiences is under their control, if they advocate for themselves and express their desires, they all too
often enter a sexual situation only to discover that—at a time
when honest communication matters the most—their genuine truth gets written off as a lie.

Every winter, as Christmas music floods the airwaves,
there's one particular song that tends to spark a bit of debate. To some listeners, it's a sweet duet about new romance;
to others, it's an uncomfortable illustration of rape culture,
codified in song. But wherever you land on it, "Baby It's Cold
Outside" is an important cultural artifact in the history of
American understanding of consent.

Written in 1944, the song has been recorded dozens of
times, by a diverse array of artists—Ella Fitzgerald, Lady
Gaga, Michael Bublé, and Willie Nelson have all put their
stamp on it at one time or another. Technically, the song
is gender neutral—the two parts are noted as "mouse" and
"wolf," rather than "woman" and "man"—and some artists
have played with the audience's gendered expectations in

their recordings of the work.[2] But in most people's minds, the song has a distinctly gendered cast. The mouse—who frets about what their family might think if they don't return home—is presumed female, while the wolf—who urges the mouse to stay regardless—is presumed male. And that presumption of gender roles is what makes the song so thorny to grapple with.

From one angle, "Baby It's Cold Outside" is a perfect illustration of the world that Barrica was raised in. A woman finds herself at the end of a delightful date, and though she'd like to take things further, she knows that if she does, she'll face the judgment of her family, community, and all polite society. And so she rejects her paramour's advances. He, in turn, persists, knowing that she'd actually love to stay if only she could craft a compelling enough cover story (that it was too cold to leave his house, that there were no cabs available, that—oops!—the drink she imbibed just got her too drunk to travel). It's a playful game of cat and mouse (well, wolf and mouse) that allows a couple to navigate the tricky maze of pursuing pleasure in a society that frowns on it, all while keeping up appearances.

But when you remove the song from that setting and put it in one where women ostensibly have the freedom to express their sexual desires, to act on them without social repercussion, it quickly becomes muddied and uncomfortable. Instead of "playing hard to get," the mouse is now offering up her mother, her neighbors, and her siblings as shields

---

[2] In 1949's *Neptune's Daughter*—the film featuring the first recordings of the song—two different couples perform the song, with the man as the aggressor in one and the woman taking on that role in the other. Lady Gaga plays the role of the wolf in the version she recorded with Joseph Gordon-Levitt for *Lady Gaga and the Muppets Holiday Spectacular*, and the TV show *Glee* offered up an all-male version featuring Darren Criss and Chris Colfer.

that will allow her to exit the situation while still being pleasant and polite—and instead of taking her at her word, the wolf persists in pressuring her to stay, possibly even spiking her drink in an attempt to render her pliable. A 2014 episode of *South Park* offers a concise commentary on how the song sounds to modern ears, dreaming up a star-studded holiday special in which the song is performed by Taylor Swift and Bill Cosby (then newly outed as a serial sexual predator who'd used incapacitating drugs to take advantage of his victims).

The tension between these two interpretations of "Baby It's Cold Outside"—along with the debate that resurfaces every time it returns to the airwaves—isn't just about a decades-old song that's fallen out of favor. We're conflicted about the song because we're still conflicted about what it means to navigate consent. We'd like to believe we're in a world where women clearly communicate sexual agency, but we're not even sure what that clear communication looks like or what, precisely, counts as consent. And we're still raising men to expect that women don't know how to say yes, that they need a little extra prodding or convincing or seduction, that at least some women still operate by the rules of "Baby It's Cold Outside," demurring in the hopes that men will continue to push just far enough to unleash the yes they've been burying deep inside.

And in a world where it feels equally possible that a woman might be clearly stating her intentions and that she might be putting up a front to preserve her reputation, it's understandable that some might seek out another method to confirm consent. If words can't be relied on, surely the body will offer guidance?

*   *   *

Sexuality researcher Meredith Chivers has dedicated her career to studying the psychological and physiological characteristics of desire and arousal, examining the way our mental
awareness of our arousal—our sense that we're turned on by
something—does, and in some cases doesn't, line up with
our physical responses to various stimuli. Some of Chivers's
more famous studies have documented the differences between male and female arousal patterns. Male sexual arousal
tends to be category-specific: if a man is straight, he sexually responds to images of women and sex between men and
women; if a man is gay, he sexually responds to images of
men and sex between men. For women, particularly straight
women, it's a bit trickier: Chivers's studies have found that
women tend to physically respond to images of sexual activity, independent of the gender of the participants and even
if it doesn't mentally arouse or leave them feeling turned on.
(Seriously: in one study, Chivers recorded women showing a
genital response to films of bonobo sex. None of the women
reported actually finding the film erotic.)

From Chivers's perspective, these findings lead to far
more questions than answers. "We don't really understand
what the mind-body relationship and integration is with respect to sexual desire and sexual arousal," she tells me. How
we experience desire and arousal depends on a complicated
combination of our physical, mental, and emotional states,
one that researchers like Chivers are still unspooling. Rather
than serve up simplistic conclusions about gender and
arousal, Chivers is much more interested in taking a deeper
dive into the ambiguity of arousal. "What is our relationship
with our body, and how does that influence our experience

of our sexuality?" she asks me, noting that questions like this are what truly drive her research.

And yet, she says, that sort of open-ended interpretation of her research "doesn't make for a great sound bite," which may explain why media coverage of her work has provided far less in the way of nuance. In January 2009, the *New York Times Magazine* profiled Chivers's research in a piece titled "What Do Women Want?," a headline that—to Chivers's continued frustration—led readers to believe that her intent was to provide a foolproof guide to ascertaining women's "true" desires.[3]

Much of the coverage of Chivers's research circles around, and sometimes outright embraces, what Chivers describes as "this really interesting and kind of repugnant idea that somehow because we measure a body—if it's a brain, if it's a vulva, if it's a clitoris, or whatever—that that is somehow closer to a truth than what somebody actually says." It's an interpretation that Chivers finds fascinating yet troubling, a gross misunderstanding of her work that nevertheless reveals a great deal about how we understand sex, the body, and the vagaries of consent.

At the base of it all, Chivers tells me, is our culture's generally misguided understanding of psychology. We have, she explains, "this idea that if something lights up in the brain, then it must be real, it must be natural," superceding any other understanding we might have of ourselves and our

---

[3] The article itself was at least somewhat more judicious in its coverage, at least when compared to a 2008 piece that ran in the *Times* Styles section, which placed Chivers's work within "a growing body of scientific evidence that places female sexuality along a continuum between heterosexuality and homosexuality, rather than as an either-or phenomenon."

identity. "And that is just false," Chivers says, noting that the division between mind and body is not nearly so clear as many of us seem to believe—and that, complicating things further, our experience within the world is also shaped by our culture and upbringing, which can affect how our mind interprets the various biological processes our body may be engaging in.

Overly simplistic (and inaccurate) as it may be, many of us still cling to the idea that the body and the mind are wholly separate entities, and whenever they happen to come into conflict, the body is the final arbiter of truth—particularly when it comes to sex. It's not difficult to understand why it's so appealing to apply this framework to an erotic context. Though sex is, at its root, a basic biological impulse, our relationship to it is complicated by layers of cultural restrictions. The notion that the body might offer a convenient shorthand allows us to cut through the confusion created by a repressive culture. Our mouths may say no to preserve our reputations and social standing, but our bodies reveal a deeper truth. I may reject someone's advances, but if my body shows signs of arousal—a lubricated vagina, erect nipples, a certain flush—that's all the proof necessary to indicate I actually wanted it.

But the notion that women's bodies offer the ultimate measure of sexual desire is a deeply flawed one. Despite our conviction that, as Shakira once said, "hips don't lie," Chivers strongly believes that "there isn't this one-to-one relationship between a body responding and people feeling aroused or feeling desire.... These physical responses are couched within all kinds of different layers." Women who suffer from persistent genital arousal disorder (PGAD)—a condition in which the body displays physical signs of arousal for hours,

days, or even endlessly, regardless of whether or not anything sexy is going on—aren't walking around constantly
looking for a fuck; to the contrary, many PGAD sufferers are
deeply distressed by their body's erotic response to utterly
unsexy and often mundane activities. Cara Anaya, a PGAD
sufferer who can experience upwards of 180 orgasms in just
a few hours, has told members of the media that her condition is "embarrassing and confusing and humiliating," noting that her constant arousal makes it hard to participate in
many everyday activities—including something as basic as
picking her son up from school.

Similarly, when women experience arousal and orgasm
during rape, it's not the body's admission that they actually
wanted the sex they did not consent to. A 2004 paper published in the *Journal of Clinical Forensic Medicine* noted that
somewhere between 4 and 5 percent of rape survivors report experiencing orgasm during rape. While many might
interpret this as an indication of an enjoyable experience,
survivors themselves tend to see it as an act of betrayal that
undermines the trauma of their experience.[4]

On the other end of the spectrum from PGAD sufferers and orgasming rape victims are women whose bodies
fail to reflect the erotic desire that's coursing through their
brains. Many women report feeling plenty of desire even
as their genitals fail to respond with the signs of physical
arousal (indeed, a thriving market for lube is a testament
to that reality). Though romance novels and erotic stories
often suggest otherwise, female sexual response is often

---

[4] Indeed, the paper's authors note that the actual number of women who experience orgasm during rape may be significantly higher than 4–5 percent, as this
shame around nonconsensually induced orgasm likely prevents women from
reporting it.

nonconcordant—a fancy way of saying that what's going on in the brain doesn't inherently match what's going on in the body.

Or, in other words, the idea that Chivers's research on physical arousal might unlock some guide to deciphering what women truly want? It's not based in reality. There are documented cases of vaginas lubricating, labia swelling, and even a female body orgasming, all without any of that registering as arousal for the brain inside that body. There are also instances of women reporting arousal and orgasm that aren't reflected by tools measuring their blood flow and brain activity. Far from being an easy-to-read manual that offers up everything one needs to know about a woman's sexual interests and arousal, the female body is often an un-reliable guide to what's actually going on inside our heads. In order to truly know what a woman wants, you have to, well, actually ask her.

It's an incredibly simple concept, but it's one that can be difficult to grapple with in a culture that routinely reinforces the message that sex is derailed by any kind of discussion—that "body language" is superior, and often preferable, to ver-bal communication. Yet bodies rarely communicate with the degree of clarity provided by the spoken word. Even when our genitals and minds are in total agreement when it comes to our level of arousal, even when we're interested in *some* degree of physical intimacy, there's still the question of how we want to experience that intimacy. The body alone has a hard time expressing whether a kiss is just a kiss or an in-vitation to something more, whether naked cuddling is the main event or just the first act of the evening. What one per-son feels is an obvious "go" sign might read as something far more vague to their partner—and until we start talking to one another, we're doomed to be mired in confusion.

Despite our conviction that the body is an authoritative guide to a partner's true desires, the body alone cannot consent to sex. "You still have a brain there," Harding tells me. "It doesn't matter how wet you are, you still have to say yes or no." The body is not a lie detector; the body does not attest to some higher truth. Truly consensual sex requires more than just physical arousal—it requires the active, enthusiastic participation of everyone involved in the act.

Barrica no longer buys into the messages she was taught by her parents. As the founder of sex education start-up O.School, she actively works to fight against them, helping young people—and young women in particular—detox from and unlearn the harmful messages that have impaired their ability to embrace and enjoy their sexuality.

At O.School, as in most progressive sex education platforms, affirmative consent is treated as the gold standard of sexual communication. Under the affirmative consent model, sex only happens if everyone involved clearly communicates an interest in proceeding. There's no need to rely on indirect methods of deciphering sexual interest—what someone was wearing, how much they laughed at your jokes, what position they contorted their body into—because if someone wants to have sex with you, they'll be up-front about it, as well as being up-front about how and when and under what circumstances they are interested in that sex taking place.

But affirmative consent is often easier said than done. It's one thing to understand that clearly, openly communicating about your needs and sexual desires increases your chances of having a mutually enjoyable sexual encounter. It's a wholly separate thing to get to the point where you're comfortable openly expressing your sexual desires—and, more importantly, actually capable of doing so.

"There's no tool to enact these basic principles of ask for what you want, and say no to what you don't want," Barrica tells me. For women, especially, the simple task of figuring out what provides them with pleasure—even just for their own edification—can feel paralyzingly complex. In her workshops, Barrica often begins by asking participants to make a list of things that give them pleasure—not a list of sexual acts they're willing to perform but a list of experiences that delight them. "My list includes getting my hair blow-dried," Barrica notes. "It doesn't have to all be overtly sexual."

And yet even that basic an exercise proves a challenge for most of Barrica's workshop participants. "No one's ever asked them what they want," says Barrica. And when asked to truly consider their own physical wants and needs, rather than their willingness to acquiesce to the desires of a partner, many women find themselves stumped.

Barrica isn't the only one who's noticed this knowledge gap among women. Writer and activist Jaclyn Friedman tells me that her book *What You Really Really Want: The Smart Girl's Shame-Free Guide to Sex and Safety* was partly inspired by the numerous women who confessed to her that they had no idea how to figure out what sexual acts they did, and did not, want to consent to. "A lot of women are growing up and coming into our sexualities subconsciously protecting ourselves from knowing what we actually do and don't want," Friedman tells me. "Because we know that it's not okay to pursue it. It's not okay to say yes or no because in the dominant culture, we're the pursued. We're the acquired sexually; we're not supposed to be the sexual actors. Violating that can come with consequences."

Even as sexually voracious women have become more socially acceptable, there are still limits to what that sexual voracity is allowed to look like. It's one thing to want to be sexy: women who relish stoking other people's sexual desire are given a fair bit of leeway publicly to perform their sexuality. But to be *sexual*, to embrace one's own desires and impulses, independent of whether or not they're interesting to, or inclusive of, men? That's not nearly so readily embraced.

Women who position themselves as active sexual consumers rather than passive sex objects are, at best, figures of fun, like *Broad City*'s Ilana Wexler or Donna from *Parks and Recreation*, and at worst, objects of aggressive scorn. When Lena Dunham dared to write a *Girls* episode in which her awkward, unsexy character, Hannah Horvath, spent a romantic weekend with a wealthy, handsome doctor, male critics reacted viciously, declaring the episode an unrealistic fantasy and (at least according to Slate) "the worst episode of *Girls* ever." Never mind that average-looking male protagonists who successfully pursue stunningly beautiful women is a standard TV trope; a female character who flips the script is deemed not merely unbelievable but outright abhorrent. In contrast, women who enthusiastically objectify themselves are often put forth as taking charge of their own sexuality, even when there's no indication that their own erotic needs are being met or even considered. Nicki Minaj's "Anaconda," which promised to flip the script on the early nineties anthem "Baby Got Back," was heralded as "the fiercest take on female sexuality of [2014]," in spite of the fact that the video for "Anaconda" offers up a one-sided vision of female sexuality, in which looking pretty and giving a capable lap dance are the only options on offer.

Barrica frames this disconnect between being sexy and feeling sexual as the difference between desire and pleasure. Women who grow up with more exposure to examples of themselves as sexual objects than of sexual subjects can often confuse the two; the thrill of having someone want to have sex with you can get confused for the experience of physically enjoying having sex—particularly when, as with "Anaconda," images of women being sexy are held up as the epitome of female sexual liberation. Barrica tells me of a Princeton student who was stunned to discover that sex even *could* be physically pleasurable for her. For all the talk of sexually liberated millennials, Barrica finds that she still spends a great deal of time explaining to women what it means to actually want to experience a sexual act rather than merely be willing to endure it.

Even seemingly basic asks—to be held, to have your hair stroked—can be difficult for young women, who don't always feel safe enough to request something that's not directly correlated to their partner's desire and orgasm. "It messes me up to see this culture," Barrica says. "It messes me up because I also experienced that: I was confusing desire for pleasure. He really desires me, or she really desires me; this is great sex."

Why is pleasure such a challenging concept for so many women? There's no one specific reason. Some of us are held back by shame that's instilled at a young age: it's hard to explore your sexuality, or learn about your body, when you're convinced that masturbation is dirty, disgusting, or an outright sin. For others, it's the lack of representation of female pleasure that leaves them stumped. When entertainment, both mainstream and erotic, routinely depicts sexual pleasure from a straight male point of view, women are forced to reverse engineer their pleasure, working backwards from male desire to construct their own experiences. And then there's the matter that, from some of their very first instances of sexual education, girls aren't taught to think of pleasure as an integrated part of their sexual development.

"What is the dominant narrative out there for girls to understand what happens when they go through puberty and they become women?" Chivers asks me. "For boys it's about, 'You're going to get erections; there's going to be these nocturnal emissions; you're going to have wet dreams.' For girls, it's 'You're going to start menstruating.' The narrative of what happens in terms of the awakening of sexual feelings, having very strong genital sensations, feeling turned on, getting lubricated, and so on—it's just missing from the dominant discourse about what happens as girls come into their sexuality." Pleasure is endemic to our narrative of male sexual development; for women, it's treated as wholly separate from the main event of reproduction.

And when women aren't taught to understand pleasure as something they themselves can access, as a fundamental biological response that's ingrained into their bodies; when they're taught to see being desired by men as an acceptable substitute for expressing their own sexual agency, it's unsurprising that they let men take the lead in sex. And when men are used to dictating how a sexual encounter unfolds, it's unsurprising that they begin to believe that their interpretation of a sexual situation is the universal, undeniable truth of what has occurred.

*   *   *

"Coercion is presented as a natural part of sexuality and of heterosexual relationships," Harding tells me. "The idea that men
are supposed to keep pushing past the woman's no is still very
much there, even though we supposedly know better now."
We're no longer in the era of "Baby It's Cold Outside," when
even the most willing woman shielded her virtue by denying her desire until suitably pushed. But the idea that women
need to be persuaded, that they're in denial about their true
desires, that their no is just a duplicitous front to increase their
desirability, is still very much in play. The trope of female resistance as a temporary obstacle that can be worn down and
overcome is everywhere: it's a central plot point in nearly
every romantic comedy, where persistent, aggressive harassment gets repackaged as persuasion, devotion, and romance.

And it shows up in the seduction strategies of many
men—sometimes even self-identified feminists who should
theoretically know better. In January 2018, feminist blog
Babe.net published an account of a date with the actor, author, and comedian Aziz Ansari, one that made Ansari seem
more like a two-bit pickup artist than a thoughtful feminist
ally who'd penned a book on modern dating.[5] In the essay's
telling, Ansari acts like a "horny, rough, entitled 18-year-
old," one who interprets "no" as "try again in a little bit,"
rather than "no, seriously, stop." When his date says she's
not ready to have sex, he agrees to take a break—only to
roughly kiss her, shove his fingers down her throat, and attempt to take her pants off.

Ansari may not have committed sexual assault, but it's
hard to see his actions as those of a man invested in his

---

[5] The latter, of course, being Ansari's public persona.

partner's pleasure. Instead, he seems to see the evening as an opportunity to take what he can get, his partner's pleasure be damned—an attitude, it should be noted, that's hardly limited to him. In a 2015 essay for *Matter*, Charlotte Shane declares her intention to "swipe right on monogamy," blaming the shitty behavior of men for her rejection of casual sex. "When arranging my 'casual encounters,' I hoped for low level warmth and good naturedness to accompany fun sex, but this modest combination was exceedingly rare," she writes, going on to declare that "being straight is a constant exercise in degradation"—even when it involves dalliances with men who talk a good game and claim to have nothing but respect for women.

For Friedman, it's not hard to see why this toxic dynamic of persistence and pressure packaged as seduction persists. To be blunt, it benefits men. "A lot of guys like the idea that no means yes because they don't want to have to think about female agency and humanity when it comes to sex," she says. "It's complicated, and it means they might get rejected. And if they get the signal that nobody's going to hold them accountable and that's okay, that's appealing." It's always easier to ask for forgiveness than to get permission. And when you can evade asking for forgiveness by leaning in to the idea that a verbal no is too ambiguous to be trusted, why put in the work required to ensure that you and your partners are truly having enthusiastic consensual sex?

We often talk about female sexual liberation as though it's just a masturbation workshop or affirmative consent law away from being realized, as though women's sexual power is accessible, if only women would just claim it. If a woman wants to have a good sex life, she need only conquer her shame and put her desires out into the world, societal

judgments be damned. But the truth of women's sexual freedom, of egalitarian, consensual, heterosexual sex, is significantly more complicated.

In its simplest definition, a sexual act can be considered
consensual when all parties involved say yes to it. Yet while
those yeses are a necessary component of consent, yeses
alone—verbally signified or otherwise—are not sufficient
assurance that a sexual encounter is consensual. Someone
who is drunk, for instance, is generally understood to be unable to meaningfully consent to sex, no matter how many
times they might insist that they're ready and willing to do
it. Age also modifies one's ability to consent to sex: a child
who propositions an adult can still be seen as a victim rather
than a consenting participant, deemed too young to fully
comprehend the impact of their actions.

Differentials in power can also add complexity to a superficially consensual relationship. There's a reason why sexual
relationships between teachers and students, or bosses and
employees, are generally frowned upon. When one party
wields control over another's education, profession, and general well-being, the boundaries between consent and coercion become increasingly fuzzy.

Harding offers another example of complicated consent,
pointing out that women who are in abusive relationships
may be choosing to engage in sex with their partners, but if
that choice is made as a way of staving off anger, or preventing a violent episode, she says, "Meaningful consent is out
the window."

"Plenty of women will have sex with a guy to calm him
down when they don't really want to," Harding continues.
"That's not exactly consensual"—though, she notes, it's not
exactly rape, either. A woman who opts to have sex because

it's preferable to being physically abused may be exercising some form of agency, but it's a limited sort that highlights her lack of power far more than it highlights her freedom of choice.

And this example of consent within an abusive dynamic offers an interesting lens through which to consider the situation of women who are, in a sense, in an abusive relationship with the patriarchy. The legacy of American women is one of significant disempowerment. It's only been in the past few decades that American women have been recognized as individuals in their own right: it wasn't that long ago that women were literally the property of either their fathers or their husbands,[6] women's ability to live their lives wholly contingent upon male approval. Writing in the May 1980 issue of *Political Theory*, Carole Pateman argues that, as a result of a long history of disempowerment, "women exemplify the individuals who consent theorists have declared are incapable of consenting," and yet, paradoxically, women are presumed to perpetually be giving consent to their partners, their husbands, even their rapists. Although we've made great strides in the decades since Pateman published her paper, women are still held back by this legacy of oppression. As the artist Emma Sulkowicz, who expounds on the flawed nature of our model of consent in "Truth Inside, Truth Outside," tells me, "Yes means yes doesn't work when you consider the historical power imbalance" between men and women.

And the current balance of power isn't much better. As Friedman explains to me, the American conception of sex—which positions men as active participants and women as passive objects—perpetuates women's sexual

---

[6] Or, in the case of enslaved women, the property of slaveholders.

disempowerment. As an illustrative example, she compares and contrasts the reactions of bystanders who witnessed the Steubenville rape and those who apprehended Brock Turner mid–sexual assault. "They asked one of the kids who was a bystander to the Steubenville rape, 'Why didn't you intervene when you saw your buddies doing this?' And he said, 'I didn't know that that was what rape looked like. I didn't know I was watching rape.'" In contrast, the Swedish men who witnessed a similar scene as they biked past Brock Turner and his victim immediately identified the encounter as a sexual assault in progress.

For Friedman, these wildly different reactions to similar incidents were born out of wildly different conceptions of what sex is supposed to look like. "[The Steubenville bystander] was raised in America, where you expect men to sexually consume passive women. That's what he saw: a woman passively being consumed by two guys," Friedman explains. "Those two Swedes on bicycles in the Brock Turner case saw literally the same scene: a woman lying passively being sexually consumed and acted upon by a guy. And they said, 'That looks wrong. We should intervene.' Because they were raised in Sweden, where they were taught affirmative consent since kindergarten. And they expect anybody engaging in sex to look like they're participating."

If sex requires two people of equal power to be considered fully consensual, and if women are systematically disempowered, both in their everyday lives and their ability to express sexual agency, then what does it really mean to have consensual heterosexual sex? I do not mean to suggest—as an apocryphal quote alternately misattributed to both Catherine MacKinnon and Andrea Dworkin states—that all heterosexual sex is rape. It's harmful to present women as permanent victims. To rob women of their agency, to negate their right to map out their sexual paths as they see fit, is not something that I'd really consider progress. But to pretend that men and women come to sexual encounters as equals seems equally foolish. We don't enter relationships on a level playing field, and to ignore the daily experience of scrutiny, harassment, and oppression that women must build their lives around does women a tremendous disservice.

To talk about affirmative consent without acknowledging this backdrop of sexist and patriarchal oppression that women must contend with is to engage in what Friedman terms "fauxpowerment." The message that female liberation is found through engaging in sexual pursuits, or that it's easily accessed by speaking up and voicing one's needs and sexual desires, "doesn't take into context that sex can be scary and that there are still an enormous number of institutions and cultural traditions that make sex really difficult for women," Friedman tells me. "The idea that you're just supposed to go out and get it leaves a lot of women feeling alienated and confused. The idea that the only obstacle to you feeling sexually fulfilled is you—it's bullshit."

"We don't need empowerment messages; we need *power*," Friedman tells me. And getting power requires more than just speaking up and explaining what it is we want; it requires more than just going out and getting our freak on. To get power, women need structural change.

"Patriarchy devalues our desires and needs and autonomy so much that we have to find ways around it," Harding tells me. Women live in a world where their pleasure is less important than a male partner's, where a man's humiliation in the face of rejection is deemed more traumatizing than the expectation that women play nice and endure unwanted sexual attention. Women are told to advocate for themselves, but when they do, men insist they don't *really* know what they want, or that men understand female desires better than women do—and that, coincidentally, women's true desires just happen to line up with whatever it is men want.

"Part of trying to stay sane in the face of being gaslit is sometimes [lying] to the people who are doing the gaslighting," Harding continues, referring to the abusive strategy of making a victim doubt their reality by insisting that falsehoods are true. Men presume to have the authoritative perspective on any situation—even ones in which they are completely out of their depth—and they badger women into believing, or at least accepting, the male perspective as the one that is unbiased and true. Women, she tells me, are all just doing their best to survive within a culture that routinely assaults them—both literally and metaphorically.

A lie is, in a sense, an attempt to claim power, and as a short-term strategy it can be a fairly successful one. A woman who fakes an orgasm because it's the only way to bring an end to a sexual encounter she's decided she's done with is, in that moment, making a perfectly rational decision. So is a woman who creates a fake boyfriend to deter a catcaller or hides her birth control use to encourage condom compliance.

But as the lies invariably add up, the situation becomes untenable. A woman who habitually lies about her lack of orgasm can end up trapping herself into a cycle of unenjoyable sexual encounters. As women lie about their relationship statuses and sexual histories to evade the judgment of those who would hold their sex lives to punishing and unfair standards, they inadvertently end up strengthening these oppressive systems by pretending to play along.

And as women lie for their own self-protection, they establish themselves as untrustworthy. The more real examples there are of women lying about sex for wholly rational reasons, the more fuel they offer to those who seek to use female dishonesty as a justification for denying women rights. These lies may begin as an earnest attempt at self-protection, but when women are at their most vulnerable, that reputation for dishonesty ultimately makes them less safe.

"Thinking about women as sexual liars absolutely leads up to enabling sexual violence," Friedman tells me. When women are established as liars, the inviolability of their boundaries is up for debate; when women are established as liars, everything they say can be called into doubt. When women are established as liars, it becomes possible to dismiss everything that comes out of their mouths as a possible, or even probable, falsehood—even in situations where it makes little to no sense for them to lie.

It feels impossible to talk about sex, lies, and consent without addressing the specter of the false rape claim—that bogeyman that haunts any woman who dares to come forward about an experience of violation or sexual abuse. In the popular imagination, women "cry rape" because they want revenge against an ex, because they had consensual sex and then regretted it, because they want attention or money or some sort of legal victory against an enemy. Even self-proclaimed feminists are susceptible to this idea. When *Girls* writer Murray Miller was publicly accused of rape by actress Aurora Perrineau, co-showrunners Lena Dunham and Jenni

Konner released a joint statement declaring that thanks to "insider knowledge" they were confident that "this accusation is one of the 3% of assault cases that are misreported every year."[7] They're hardly alone in abandoning the rallying cry of "Believe women" as soon as it means believing something bad about a male friend.

While false rape accusations and charges are a documented (albeit rare) occurrence, the reality of who lies about rape is significantly different from the popular conception. In an essay for *Quartz*, Sandra Newman summarizes the existing research on false rape charges, noting that—unlike rape survivors, who come from every conceivable background and demographic—people who file false rape claims tend to fit a very specific profile. According to Newman, "adult[8] false accusers who persist in pursuing charges have a previous history of bizarre fabrications or criminal fraud.... They're often criminals whose family and friends are also criminals; broken people trapped in chaotic lives." They're also very likely to put forth allegations that are in line with our collective understanding of a "real" rape: Newman notes that "in a study of false rape claims made to the Los Angeles Police Department, 78% involved claims of aggravated

---

[7] A statement rendered even more tone-deaf given that, just a few months prior, Dunham had tweeted that women don't lie about rape. Dunham apologized shortly after defending Miller, releasing a second statement on Twitter telling fans and followers that "I naively believed it was important to share my perspective on my friend's situation as it has transpired behind the scenes over the last few months. I now understand that it was absolutely the wrong time to come forward with such a statement and I am so sorry."

[8] Newman specifies "adult" here to differentiate these accusers from teenage accusers, who are more likely to invent a rape as an alibi or to avoid getting in trouble for consensual sex, and only involve the police when their parents insist on escalating the situation.

rape—assaults involving a gun or knife, gang rapes, and/or attacks resulting in injuries."

"The stories told in false accusations tend to be about stranger rapes with weapons because we know what people are more likely to believe," Harding tells me. When women lie about rape, they are unlikely to put forth complicated stories of ambiguous consent. The prominent stories that attract the most doubt—tales of an initially consensual encounter gone horribly awry or anecdotes about a drunken night ending in unwanted sex—are the least likely to be false. No one determined to destroy someone's reputation with a false report of rape is likely to present themselves as an imperfect victim, or give their audience any reason to doubt that they are, in fact, telling the truth. Muddying the waters with tales of consent that was given and then withdrawn does little to serve the strategic end goal of a lie.

And lies are strategic. Whether they are faking their orgasms or inventing boyfriends or concealing their pasts, women lie for specific reasons, ones that are often deeply connected to their very survival. Women lie because society won't accept their truth, and they lie because their truth puts them at risk; they lie because sometimes a socially approved falsehood is the only reasonable way forward. Women lie because sometimes a lie is the only way to express a deeper truth. As Aliza Shvarts, who researched documented instances of false rape allegations for one of her works, tells me, these lies may not be specifically about rape, certainly not in the way it is described to police, but they are an attempt to express a very real violation and hurt. "What truth is being testified to in the false rape report that can't be expressed otherwise?" Shvarts asks me. In a different conversation, Friedman offers up a sentiment that parallels Shvarts's, telling me that "if someone tells you they feel violated, they're telling you that they are profoundly injured." Even the falsest of rape claims is, at its core, a testament to the deep and lasting trauma of being a woman in a culture that systematically devalues and disbelieves her.

In our fixation on female dishonesty, we tend to focus on what these lies tell us about women, rather than what these lies tell us about society. But a deep look at the reasons and rationale behind female dishonesty offers up the most surprising truth of all. Women lie because they're told, over and over again, that their truths are an impossibility. And—perhaps paradoxically—the best way to combat these ever-present falsehoods, the best way to get women to stop lying in the first place, is with trust, respect, and, above all, belief.

Believing It

I FIRST HEARD about Emma Sulkowicz in the fall of 2014. At the time, Sulkowicz was a student at Columbia University, embarking on an ambitious performance project. Sulkowicz, who felt that their[1] report of rape had been handled improperly, first by the university's official reporting channels and later by the NYPD, chose to seek reparation through art. And thus *Mattress Performance (Carry That Weight)* was born.

The idea behind *Mattress Performance (Carry That Weight)* was a simple one. Sulkowicz's trauma was a constant mental burden for them. *Mattress Performance (Carry That Weight)* transformed that burden into a literal, physical one, requiring Sulkowicz to lug a fifty-pound mattress—the same make and model as the one they'd been assaulted on—everywhere they went on campus, for the rest of their time at Columbia, or until their assailant left campus.

Sulkowicz had always assumed that the project would garner attention on campus, but they never anticipated the degree to which it would capture the attention of the press. By the end of September, *Mattress Performance (Carry That Weight)* had been written up by the *New York Times*, *New York Magazine*, *Elle*, Artnet, and MSNBC; even Hillary

---

[1] Sulkowicz uses nonbinary pronouns.

Clinton addressed it, briefly mentioning the project in a speech at the Democratic National Committee Women's Leadership Forum Conference. The *New York Post*, the *New York Daily News*, *Jezebel*, *Mic*, the *New Yorker*, *Breitbart*, the *National Review*: everyone seemed to have an opinion on the story, and everyone was eager to share it. As the coverage accumulated, Sulkowicz transformed into a symbol of the national discussion on rape. Depending on your perspective, they were either a brave hero willing to endure pain and public scrutiny in an effort to push the issue of campus sexual assault into the national discourse or a self-obsessed, attention-hungry narcissist willing to exploit the tragedy endured by "real" rape victims in order to get attention. *New York Magazine* described the work as "radical vulnerability"; the *National Review* derided Sulkowicz as a "pitiable poet" who embodied the "intellectual selfishness" of the feminist left.

When I first reached out to Sulkowicz, I assumed that they'd repeat the same refrain I had heard so often, from so many women and survivors of sexual assault: We must believe women. We must trust women. The cost of coming forward is too high to do on a whim; anyone willing to endure the retraumatization, the public humiliation, that Sulkowicz had been put through must be coming from an authentic place of victimization and hurt.

It didn't quite work out like that.

"There's one type of feminism in which you try and reverse the power structure," Sulkowicz tells me over lunch at a Union Square café. That kind of feminism, Sulkowicz notes, can best be thought of as a "feminism of empowerment." It's the strategy most often employed by prominent, mainstream feminists who pen think pieces and do college speaking tours, putting forth data-driven arguments for the eradication of the patriarchy. It's the strategy of social media campaigns that implore women to share their stories, to create a critical mass of experience that can no longer be dismissed as vengeful fabrication. Sulkowicz supports that strategy and has, at times, employed it in their work. But they're also attracted to another kind of feminism, one that's less promoted but perhaps more feasible: "It's about finding power in the position of disempowerment," Sulkowicz tells me, describing the tactic as "a self-destructive and productive turn inwards."

It's the latter form of engagement that Sulkowicz has readily embraced in the years since *Mattress Performance (Carry That Weight)*. "Would I really agree that the project of my artwork is to make women more believable?" they muse over lunch. "I'm wondering if it's kind of shoving in your face how unbelievable I am. I'm never really trying to prove to you that I'm believable."

Sulkowicz's follow-up to *Mattress Performance (Carry That Weight)* was an explicit[2] attempt to push the boundaries of "believability," to put the lie to every self-appointed expert who dismissed their victimhood and denied their accounting of rape. In the aftermath of *Mattress Performance (Carry That Weight)*, they'd been dogged by self-declared experts who felt justified in weighing in on the veracity of Sulkowicz's statements. There were internet commenters who endlessly debated Sulkowicz's victim status, journalists who sought to debunk their account of events, and even something of a counter–art protest, in the form of posters featuring a photo

---

[2] Literally.

of Sulkowicz alongside the phrase "Pretty Little Liar," which appeared all across the Columbia campus just hours after Sulkowicz's graduation. Sulkowicz couldn't have been raped, commentators argued, because they'd initially consented to sex. They couldn't have been raped because they didn't have enough visible bruises or physical trauma after the assault. They couldn't have been raped because they continued a superficially friendly correspondence with their alleged assailant, something presumably unfathomable for a sexual assault survivor. Or to put all these points more succinctly: Sulkowicz could not have been raped because they had failed to conform to our collective idea of how a "real" sexual assault victim dresses, looks, and acts.

Sulkowicz's response was twofold. They wanted, first, to create an art piece that forced their audience of rape "experts" to directly confront the ugliness of sexual assault in a way that stripped away any preconceptions of what violation is and is not. And they wanted to challenge the persistent notion that "real" rape survivors respond to their violation in one specific way, since, they tell me, "real rape survivors are infinitely capable human beings."

In order to accomplish those twin goals, they decided to push the boundaries of acceptable postrape behavior with a work that violently refuses to conform to expectation. "What's the one thing a 'real' rape survivor would never do?" they ask. "I decided that the one thing a real rape survivor would never do is do it again. And put it online."

The resulting work, *Ceci N'est Pas Un Viol*,[3] is an eight-minute video that has been described, in various press outlets, as "a disturbing sex tape," "unsettling and thought-provoking,"

---

[3] Sulkowicz tells me that the original title was *The Proof I Wish I Had*.

and "troubling."[4] The video is prefaced with an artist's statement that invites the audience to think deeply about their motivations for engaging with the work. "Are you searching for proof? Proof of what?" the statement asks. "Do you think I'm the perfect victim or the world's worst victim?" The answers to these questions, it's implied, say far more about the viewer—and about society as a whole—than they do about Sulkowicz.

In some tellings of this story, Emma Sulkowicz is a liar: an archetypal example of the woman who, fueled by regret or inexplicable desire for revenge, turns to accusations of rape in an attempt to ruin a man's reputation. That's the version of the story peddled by the *Daily Beast* in an essay titled "Columbia Student: I Didn't Rape Her," in which Sulkowicz's alleged assailant, Paul Nungesser, attempts to clear his name. That's the version of the story implicitly endorsed by Columbia University's decision to settle a Title IX lawsuit filed by Nungesser, who argued that, by allowing Sulkowicz to carry out their project on campus, the university had violated his rights.

That's not the version of the story that I believe. As the pages of this book have detailed, when women lie, they tend to do so for a strategic and thoughtful reason. Rarely, if ever, is that reason to thrust themselves into the national limelight, to open themselves up to abuse and humiliation, to invite millions of strangers to scrutinize their every outfit, experience, and turn of phrase. Far more often, the lie about sex is one intended to eschew, rather than invite, attention. Women fake an orgasm to put a stop to someone's badgering;

---

[4] By Jezebel, Bustle, and Artnet, respectively.

they invent a boyfriend to dissuade a would-be suitor; they feign sexual purity to reinforce the strength of their relationships. Even lies about sexual assault are, in most cases, lies intended to evade punishment, not to bring it on in the form of endless online harassment.

But in telling their truth, Sulkowicz nonetheless offers insight into the particulars of why it is that women are drawn to falsehood. Sulkowicz tried, multiple times, to go through the proper channels. They tried speaking directly to Nungesser, to see if any sort of amends could be made. They tried reporting the assault to Columbia University, only to have their account of rape declared insufficiently convincing. They attempted to seek justice from the police but found them to be dismissive. It was only after these repeated refusals that Sulkowicz chose to get creative; it was only after being told, time and again, that their reality could not be real that Sulkowicz began to explore how easy it can be to blur the boundaries between truth and fiction. The deceptions that women embrace are a form of the feminism of disempowerment that Sulkowicz now champions. When women's truths are denied, they have no recourse but to turn to a socially acceptable fiction; when the only means to achieve their ends are laced with falsehood, women embrace that means because they have to.

Sulkowicz acknowledges that there's a version of this story in which *Mattress Performance (Carry That Weight)* never happened. "If Paul had just apologized, I wouldn't have had to make art, because then it would have been, 'Oh, he understands that he fucked up, and he probably won't do it again,'" they tell me. But when that never happened, they realized, "Okay, the message isn't getting through to him."

Nungesser certainly isn't the only one for whom the message isn't getting through. We exist in a society that still treats men as inherently trustworthy and women as inherently suspect, one in which the masculine perspective is generally deemed the unbiased and authoritative one. And it seems worth asking: What might the world look like if we actually believed women?

On October 5, 2017, the *New York Times* published an exposé of powerful Hollywood executive Harvey Weinstein, detailing decades of sexual harassment and settlements crafted to make numerous accusations disappear. A few days later, the *New Yorker* followed suit with a piece by Ronan Farrow, this one upping the charges against Weinstein from harassment to full-on rape. Initially, it all felt like business as usual: Weinstein lawyered up, all but denying the accusations with a halfhearted apology that cited the culture of his youth as a contributing factor to his predation of women. Famous friends lined up to defend him, noting that he'd always been kind to them and thus the accusations couldn't possibly be true.

But then, suddenly, something felt different. Weinstein was fired from his own company. His lawyer deserted him. His allies apologized for coming to his defense. And—at first slowly, and then in a rapid, overwhelming rush—women started to come forward about other abusers, publicly accusing a seemingly endless list of prominent men across a variety of industries of acts ranging from crude comments or a stray grope to nonconsensual exhibitionism and brutal, violent rape. In some cases, the accusations were public confirmation of long-standing "open secrets" that had followed these men for years; in other cases, they were genuinely shocking reveals.

Most shocking of all, however, was how many of these accusations were accepted as fact. Louis CK, who'd long denied rumors about his abusive proclivities, publicly acknowledged a habit of masturbating in front of women without their consent. TV showrunner Dan Harmon engaged in a very public back-and-forth with a former employee who'd accused him of sexual harassment, a conversation that culminated in a seven-minute apology on an episode of Harmon's podcast. With rare exception, women who came forward about abusers were treated as truth tellers—not after decades of pushback or being joined by dozens of other accusers but, for the most part, as soon as they saw fit to publicly share their stories.

What precipitated such a dramatic shift? To some, it seemed clear that this wave of admissions was part of a backlash to the current presidential administration, a feminist uprising in response to the presidency of Donald Trump. During a panel on women in Hollywood at the first ever Women's Convention, actress Amber Tamblyn[5] noted that, had 2017 seen the inauguration of a President Hillary Clinton, it was unlikely that this torrent of feminist fury would have been unleashed. "It took somebody as vile as Donald Trump to allow these things to start bubbling to the surface, even though it's been there all along," Tamblyn told attendees. "This has been in our country for a long time, but it took someone like him for us all to be able to point and go, 'That. That is everything that is wrong with masculinity.'"

---

[5] Who, presciently, had penned a *New York Times* op-ed detailing her experiences of harassment in the entertainment industry mere weeks before the Weinstein allegations were published.

For others, however, the outings of the fall of 2017 seemed to come from somewhere even further back. In an op-ed slamming Woody Allen for referring to sexual assault allegations as a "witch hunt," Lindy West notes that, "In the past five years there has been a positive deluge of victims speaking out—an uncountable number that represents not just the acute trauma of an unwanted touch or a dehumanizing comment, but the invisible ripples of confidence lost, jobs quit, careers stalled, women's influence diminished, men's power entrenched." For others, it wasn't a matter of years, but decades; the fall of 2017 was the culmination of a movement that had been building for decades, ever since an attorney and academic pushed the phrase "sexual harassment" into the common parlance.

"Sexual harassment issues that are being talked about now started really with Anita Hill," Michael Kimmel, professor of sociology and gender studies at SUNY Stony Brook, tells me, positioning the woman who accused Supreme Court justice Clarence Thomas as the mother of a modern movement.

Admittedly, Hill was far less successful in her pursuit of justice than modern accusers. "When she spoke, everybody said she was lying. She was a woman scorned, she was 'nutty and slutty,'" Kimmel notes, citing a slur lobbed at Hill by the writer David Brock. But in spite of her failure to unseat Thomas, Hill is a figure of significant cultural importance, Kimmel tells me. Despite a vicious campaign to discredit her, Hill still managed to inspire many other women to come forward with their own stories of abuse and assault—if not publicly, then privately, sharing their experiences with friends, family, and colleagues who might benefit from a bit of warning about a particularly dangerous man.

In the two and a half decades since Hill took the stand at Thomas's confirmation hearings, a number of women have been inspired to speak out publicly about their own assaults. And with each accusation, we've edged closer and closer to a tipping point where denial is no longer a possibility. And now, Kimmel tells me, "I think that we are at a watershed moment when women are actually being believed."

Whether the moment holds still remains to be seen. My conversation with Kimmel transpires just hours after Louis CK issued an apology for years of harassing women; even at this historic moment, Kimmel notes that he still fears a backlash. Maybe, he muses, there will be so many accusations that that harassment will begin to seem normalized. Or perhaps men will find a way to make their pervasive predatory behavior about women's actions rather than about their own.

But I hope that doesn't happen. The stakes are just too high. There is no question that women cannot be safe unless they are believed. And women will always lie so long as it's the one thing that ensures their safety.

Acknowledgments

THE IDEA FOR *Faking It* came out of an essay I penned for *Fusion* (now *Splinter News*) on our bizarre obsession with female dishonesty. I'm deeply grateful to Danielle Friedman for helping to shape that piece and putting me on the road to exploring this topic in much greater depth. I'm also incredibly indebted to my agent, Monika Verma, who pushed me to refine my argument even further; my editor, Stephanie Knapp, whose feedback has been essential; and the entire team at Seal Press for helping to bring this book out into the world.

Thanks also to Mom, Abba, Yael, and Dave for putting up with my bullshit for three decades and change, and to Kwame, for always keeping me honest.

Notes

Introduction

xiii   **the more honest and trustworthy candidate:** Scott Clement and Emily Guskin, "*Post*-ABC Tracking Poll Finds Race Tied, as Trump Opens Up an 8-Point Edge on Honesty," *Washington Post*, November 2, 2016, www.washingtonpost.com/news/the-fix/wp/2016/11/02/tracking-poll-finds-race-tied-as-trump-opens-up-an-8-point-edge-on-honesty.

xiii   **Trump told the whole, unvarnished truth just 4 percent of the time:** "Donald Trump's File," Politifact, www.politifact.com/personalities/donald-trump, accessed December 27, 2017.

xiii   **compared to Clinton's 24 percent:** "Hillary Clinton's File," Politifact, www.politifact.com/personalities/hillary-clinton, accessed December 27, 2017.

xiii   **"fundamentally honest and trustworthy.":** Jill Abramson, "This May Shock You: Hillary Clinton Is Fundamentally Honest," *Guardian*, March 28, 2016, www.theguardian.com/commentisfree/2016/mar/28/hillary-clinton-honest-transparency-jill-abramson.

Chapter One

1   **TMZ succinctly put it:** "Caitlyn Jenner: Watch Me Fake an Orgasm!," TMZ, April 11, 2016, www.tmz.com/2016/04/11/caitlyn-jenner-faking-orgasm-video.

3   **"typical" female sexual response cycle:** William Masters and Virginia Johnson, *Human Sexual Response* (Boston: Little, Brown, 1966).

4   **circular rather than linear models:** Beverly Whipple,
    "Women's Sexual Pleasure and Satisfaction: A New View of
    Female Sexual Function," *Female Patient* 27 (2002): 39–44.

4   **models that include desire:** Helen Singer Kaplan, *Disorders
    of Desire and Other New Concepts and Techniques in Sex Therapy*
    (New York: Brunner/Hazel, 1979).

4   **emotional intimacy, and other nonphysical aspects of
    sexual pleasure:** Rosemary Basson, "Female Sexual Response:
    The Role of Drugs in the Management of Sexual Dysfunction,"
    Obstetrics & Gynecology 98, no. 3 (September 2001): 522.

5   **"a gentle tingly sort of tickle":** Peter Mayle, *Where Did I
    Come From?: The Facts of Life Without Any Nonsense and with
    Illustrations* (Secaucus, NJ: Lyle Stewart, 1975), 16.

5   **"a tremendous big lovely shiver":** Ibid., 20.

6   **Mayle follows up with an aside:** Ibid.

7   **"grow wings, defy gravity":** "Chloe Thurlow Quotes,"
    GoodReads, www.goodreads.com/author/quotes/897415.Chloe
    _Thurlow?page=6.

7   **"searing heat, electric pulses surging":** Simone Freier,
    *Birthday Experience: A Celebration of Openness and Submission
    Among Adventurous Friends* (Sacramento: OTK Publications,
    2014), 95.

7   **"something blossomed deep within":** Mary Balogh, *Simply
    Magic* (New York: Delacorte, 2007), 374.

7   **surveying women about their experience of the big O:** Zoe
    Ruderman, "What the Big O Feels Like for Me," *Cosmopolitan*,
    August 29, 2016, www.cosmopolitan.com/sex-love/advice/g1551
    /what-an-orgasm-feels-like.

9   **posted in the LiveJournal community Vagina Pagina:**
    "Is This an Orgasm?," Vagina Pagina, posted May 6, 2012,
    vaginapagina.livejournal.com/20879489.html#ixzz4HnXAGMl2.

11 **"orgasm is the sudden, involuntary release of sexual
    tension,":** Emily Nagoski, *Come As You Are: The Surprising New
    Science That Will Transform Your Sex Life* (New York: Simon &
    Schuster, 2015), 267.

15 **15 percent of women find themselves unable to orgasm:**
    R. C. Rosen, "Prevalence and Risk Factors of Sexual Dysfunction
    in Men and Women," *Current Psychiatry Reports* (June 2000):
    189–195.

18   **a 2013 essay for *xoJane*:** Alana Massey, "I've Never Had an
     Orgasm and I'm the Only Person That Doesn't Care," *xoJane*,
     March 19, 2013, www.xojane.com/sex/ive-never-had-an-orgasm
     -and-im-the-only-person-that-doesnt-care.

20   **they've been pressured into sex and hope a feigned climax:**
     Emily J. Thomas, Monika Stelzl, and Michelle N. Lafrance,
     "Faking to Finish: Women's Accounts of Feigning Sexual Pleasure
     to End Unwanted Sex," *Sexualities* 20, no. 3 (March 2017):
     281–301.

20   **faking orgasm "affords some control":** "Faking to Finish—
     Women Feign Sexual Pleasure to End 'Bad' Sex," EurekAlert!,
     July 8, 2016, www.eurekalert.org/pub_releases/2016-07/bps
     -ftf070816.php.

24   **a full 25 percent of male participants had faked:** C. L.
     Muehlenhard and S. K. Shippee, "Men's and Women's Reports of
     Pretending Orgasm," *Journal of Sex Research* (November 2010):
     552–567.

25   **An interview the *Village Voice* conducted:** Foster Kamer,
     "Why Men Fake Orgasms, by a Man Who Has Faked an Orgasm,"
     Village Voice, November 8, 2010, www.villagevoice.com/2010/11
     /08/why-men-fake-orgasms-by-a-man-who-has-faked-an-orgasm.

Chapter Two

29   **"I date younger men,":** "Cindy Gallop: Make Love, Not Porn,"
     TED Talks, December 2, 2009, blog.ted.com/cindy_gallop_ma
     /comment-page-3.

32   **Personal essays lamenting the lackluster sexual
     encounters:** Rose Surnow, "Stop Trying to Choke Me: The Rise
     of Rough Sex Culture," *Elle*, May 5, 2016, www.elle.com/life-love
     /sex-relationships/news/a36150/effects-of-porn-on-sex.

32   **A *Time* magazine cover story from March 2016:** Belinda
     Luscombe, "Porn and the Threat to Virility," *Time*, March 31,
     2016, time.com/4277510/porn-and-the-threat-to-virility/?iid
     =toc_033116.

32   **their 2016 national platform:** Tal Kopan, "GOP Platform Draft
     Declares Pornography 'Public Health Crisis,'" CNN, July 11, 2016,
     www.cnn.com/2016/07/11/politics/gop-platform-republican
     -convention-internet-pornography/index.html.

36 **[Footnote 5] Titles from the nominees list:** "2018 Nominees,"
AVN Awards, avn.com/awards/nominees, accessed February 2,
2018.

37 **Bonnie Rotten won the coveted Female Performer of the
Year award:** Peter Warren, "Beyond Alt: 2014 Female Performer
of the Year Bonnie Rotten," *AVN*, March 25, 2014, avn.com
/business/articles/video/beyond-alt-2014-female-performer-of
-the-year-bonnie-rotten-553042.html.

37 **mainstream directors like Dana Vespoli:** *Girl/Boy*, Evil Angel,
October 2, 2013, www.evilangel.com/es/movie/Girl-Boy/22266.

40 **"There's a time and a place for everything,":** Ian Kerner,
She Comes First: The Thinking Man's Guide to Pleasuring a Woman
(New York: ReganBooks, 2004), 176.

40 **"You may have been too rough, or overzealous,":** Kerner, *She
Comes First*, 110.

41 **sampling of cunnilingus-related advice:** Cosmo Frank, "7 Hot
Ways to Enjoy Receiving Oral Sex," *Cosmopolitan*, December 11,
2013, www.cosmopolitan.com/sex-love/advice/a17017/let-guys
-go-down-on-you.

44 **Anne Koedt declared the vaginal orgasm to be a "myth,":**
Anne Koedt, "The Myth of the Vaginal Orgasm," in *Notes from
the Second Year: Women's Liberation—Major Writings of the Radical
Feminists* (New York: Radical Feminism, 1970).

45 **A chapter of Tim Ferriss's:** Tim Ferriss, "The Fifteen Minute
Female Orgasm—Part Deux," *The 4-Hour Body: An Uncommon
Guide to Rapid Fat Loss, Incredible Sex, and Becoming Superhuman*
(New York: Crown Archetype, 2010), 237–252.

Chapter Three

56 **[Footnote 2] a 2010 survey of Swedish health care
providers:** Birgitta Essén, Anna Blomkvist, Lotti Helström, and
Sara Johnsdotter, "The Experience and Responses of Swedish
Health Professionals to Patients Requesting Virginity Restoration
(Hymen Repair)," *Reproductive Health Matters* 18, no. 35 (May
2010): 38–46.

57 **Brelyn Bowman began popping up in the media:** Terri
Pous, "This Bride's 'Certificate of Purity' Is Causing a Huge
Debate Online," *BuzzFeed*, October 21, 2015, www.buzzfeed.com

/terripous/this-brides-certificate-of-purity-is-causing-a-massive
-debat.

57   **Elizabeth Raine threw her own V-card onto the market:**
Interview with Elizabeth Raine, March 2014, web.archive.org
/web/20140328174556/www.elizabeth-raine.com/my_interview
.html.

57   **[Footnote 4] announcing her decision to cancel the
auction:** E. J. Dickson, "27-year-old Medical Student Cancels
Her Virginity Auction After $801,000 Bid," *Daily Dot*, May 8,
2014, www.dailydot.com/irl/elizabeth-raine-auction-canceled.

62   **"a functionless leftover,":** Hanne Blank, *Virgin: The Untouched
History* (New York: Bloomsbury, 2007), 23.

62   **"a hymen is what's left over when you dig a hole.":** Blank,
Virgin, 32.

63   **Andreas Vesalius "discovered" the hymen:** Blank, *Virgin*,
50–51.

63   **"we became aware of hymens":** Blank, *Virgin*, 24.

64   **Columbia University's health Q & A site:** "Questioning
Girlfriend's Virginity," Go Ask Alice!, goaskalice.columbia.edu
/answered-questions/questioning-girlfriends-virginity, accessed
February 2, 2018.

69   **"one's first-time sexual experience is more than just a
milestone":** C. Veronica Smith and Matthew J. Shaffer, "Gone
but Not Forgotten: Virginity Loss and Current Sexual Satisfaction,"
Journal of Sex and Marital Therapy 39, no. 2 (2013): 96–111.

Chapter Four

80   **women who wear makeup at work make more money:**
Valentina Zarya, "How a Little Lipstick Could Add Thousands to
Your Paycheck," *Fortune*, May 19, 2016, fortune.com/2016/05/19
/makeup-more-money.

81   **"makeup has a beneficial impact":** Rebecca Nash, George
Fieldman, Trevor Hussey, Jean-Luc Lévêque, and Patricia
Pineau, "Cosmetics: They Influence More Than Caucasian
Female Facial Attractiveness," *Journal of Applied Social Psychology*
36, no. 2 (February 2006): 493–504.

81   **makeup artist Andreigha Wazny posted two photos:**
Andreigha Wazny (@makeupbydreigh), "My Regular," Instagram,
January 16, 2015, www.instagram.com/p/x8H3MCJVl_.

81 **Twitter user reposted them with the caption:** EL Lobo
    Negròn (@h_menace), Twitter, February 15, 2015, twitter.com
    /H_menace/status/566969147146637312.

83 **"an ode to natural beauty":** Ali Eaves, "11 Reasons Women
    Look Gorgeous Without Makeup," *Men's Health*, March 24, 2015,
    www.menshealth.com/sex-women/why-women-are-beautiful
    -without-makeup.

85 **As Rachel Bloom performs "The Sexy Getting Ready
    Song,":** "Crazy Ex-Girlfriend | The Sexy Getting Ready Song |
    The CW," YouTube, October 14, 2015, www.youtube.com/watch?v
    =hkfSDSfxE4o.

86 **[Footnote 3] An essay penned by Jessica Leigh Hester:**
    Jessica Leigh Hester, "How Concealer Covers Up Women's
    Labor," *Atlantic*, February 17, 2017, www.theatlantic.com/health
    /archive/2017/02/ready-set-gorgeous/515997.

88 **more nonblack women than women with afros:** "See Every
    King Magazine Cover," *King*, February 19, 2015, king-mag.com
    /see-every-king-magazine-cover.

89 **Jenner speaks openly about her use of lip fillers:** Bee
    Shapiro, "Kylie Jenner's Beauty Routine: How She Keeps It Real,"
    New York Times, September 8, 2015, www.nytimes.com/2015/09
    /10/fashion/kylie-jenner-beauty-regimen.html.

90 **a twenty-four-point list:** Danielle Tullo, "The 24 Meanest Things
    Celebrities Have Said About the Kardashians," *Cosmopolitan*, April
    4, 2016, www.cosmopolitan.com/entertainment/celebs/news
    /a44747/mean-things-celebrities-have-said-about-the-kardashians.

90 **a biting op-ed that opened with the author declaring:**
    Allison Pearson, "Kim Kardashian and the Price of Preening
    Narcissism," *Telegraph* (London), October 4, 2016, www
    .telegraph.co.uk/women/life/kim-kardashian-and-the-price-of
    -preening-narcissism.

91 **When asked about her talents:** "Kim Kardashian Attributes
    Career to Social Media," *CBS News*, October 21, 2016, www
    .cbsnews.com/news/kim-kardashian-social-media-career-60
    -minutes.

91 **Some of the shades sold out within mere minutes:** Clare
    O'Connor, "Kim Kardashian West Beauty Sold Out of Contour Kits
    in Less Than Three Hours," *Forbes*, June 21, 2017, www.forbes
    .com/sites/clareoconnor/2017/06/21/kim-kardashian-west

-beauty-sold-out-of-contour-kits-in-less-than-three-hours
/#1d08174b5b30.

92   **took to the Lena Dunham–backed newsletter** *Lenny Letter*:
       Alicia Keys, "Alicia Keys: Time to Uncover," *Lenny Letter*,
       May 31, 2016, www.lennyletter.com/story/alicia-keys-time-to
       -uncover.

92   **Mila Kunis, who appeared sans makeup:** Cindi Leive, "Mila
       Kunis Wears No Makeup on *Glamour*'s August 2016 Cover,"
       Glamour, July 6, 2016, www.glamour.com/story/i-love-makeup
       -i-also-love-taking-it-off.

93   **[Footnote 6] And it remains unclear just how makeup-free:**
       Maya Allen, "Here's What Happened When I Tried Alicia Keys's
       No-Makeup Makeup Routine," *Cosmopolitan*, October 7, 2016, www
       .cosmopolitan.com/style-beauty/beauty/a5086477/i-tried-alicia
       -keys-no-makeup-products.

94   **10 percent of women who live with polycystic ovary
       syndrome:** "Polycystic Ovary Syndrome," Office on Women's
       Health, US Department of Health and Human Services, www
       .womenshealth.gov/a-z-topics/polycystic-ovary-syndrome,
       accessed February 2, 2018.

95   **upwards of 40 percent of women have some sort of facial
       hair:** Julie Bindel, "Women: Embrace Your Facial Hair!,"
       Guardian (London), August 20, 2010, www.theguardian.com
       /lifeandstyle/2010/aug/20/women-facial-hair.

95   **determined by the woman's race:** Emilia Javorsky, Alexis
       C. Perkins, Greg Hillebrand, Kukizo Miyamoto, and Alexa
       Boer Kimball, "Race, Rather Than Skin Pigmentation, Predicts
       Facial Hair Growth in Women," *Journal of Clinical and Aesthetic
       Dermatology* 7, no. 5 (May 2014): 24–26.

95   **A 2013 poll conducted by Oxygen Media:** Sadie Whitelocks,
       "Mustaches on Women Revealed to Be the Ultimate Dating Turn-
       Off for Single Men (but Guys Won't Stand a Chance If They Have
       Bad Body Odor)," *Daily Mail* (London), April 10, 2013, www
       .dailymail.co.uk/femail/article-2306879/Mustaches-women
       -revealed-ultimate-dating-turn-single-men-guys-wont-stand
       -chance-bad-body-odor.html.

96   **wide-eyed estimates of how much the athlete turned
       reality star:** Mariah Haas and Nicole Sands, "Caitlyn Jenner's
       Facial Feminization Surgery: All About the Procedure—and What

It Involves," *People*, June 2, 2015, people.com/celebrity/caitlyn
-jenner-facial-feminization-surgery-costs-35000-estimates-doctor.

96   **Tabloids have detailed an array of rarely discussed
surgeries:** Steve Dorfman, "Understanding Caitlyn Jenner's
Facial Feminization Surgery," *Palm Beach Post*, July 20, 2015,
www.palmbeachpost.com/lifestyles/understanding-caitlyn
-jenner-facial-feminization-surgery/7MsOAJReEigAg6rZSpY7EP.

101   **Jenna Wortham once wrote:** Jenna Wortham, "My Selfie,
Myself," *New York Times*, October 19, 2013, www.nytimes.com
/2013/10/20/sunday-review/my-selfie-myself.html.

104   **Hess has written at length about her experiences:** Amanda
Hess, "Why Women Aren't Welcome on the Internet," *Pacific
Standard*, January 6, 2014, psmag.com/social-justice/women
-arent-welcome-internet-72170.

Chapter Five

108   **a 2013 article that appeared on *xoJane*:** Alecia Lynn
Eberhardt, "Stop Saying 'I Have a Boyfriend' to Deflect
Unwanted Attention," *xoJane*, September 9, 2013, www.xojane
.com/relationships/stop-saying-i-have-a-boyfriend.

109   **The most extreme reaction I encountered was a viral
prank:** Clementine Ford, "Rejecting a Man's Advances with 'I'm
Sorry, I Have a Boyfriend'," *Sydney Morning Herald*, November
17, 2015, www.smh.com.au/lifestyle/news-and-views/women-of
-the-year/rejecting-a-mans-advances-with-im-sorry-i-have-a
-boyfriend-20151116-gl07ah.html.

111   **a 2015 analysis from dating site OkCupid:** Kelly Cooper, "A
Woman's Advantage," OkCupid, March 5, 2015, theblog.okcupid
.com/a-womans-advantage-82d5074dde2d.

116   **a blog post from pickup coach the Modern Man:** Dan Bacon,
"How to Talk to a Woman Who Is Wearing Headphones," The
Modern Man, www.themodernman.com/dating/how-to-talk-to-a
-woman-who-is-wearing-headphones.html, accessed February 2,
2018.

120   **"I eventually find myself talking to one":** Brock Turner
defendant statement, assets.documentcloud.org/documents
/2854904/Defendantstatement.pdf, accessed February 2, 2018.

120   **a Stanford student found guilty of three felony counts:**
Hannah Knowles, "Brock Turner Found Guilty on Three Felony

Counts," *Stanford Daily*, March 30, 2016, www.stanforddaily.com /2016/03/30/brock-turner-found-guilty-on-three-felony-counts.

120 **In the essay "D,":** Jessica Valenti, *Sex Object* (New York: Dey Street Books, 2016), 125–130.

126 **In a 1980 essay:** Dolores Hayden, "What Would a Non-Sexist City Be Like? Speculations on Housing, Urban Design, and Human Work," *Signs* 5, no. 3 (Spring 1980): S170–S187.

126 **many public transportation systems were initially designed:** Ankita Rao, "Sexism and the City," *Vice*, May 16, 2017, www.vice.com/en_id/article/d7a55a/sexism-and-the-city-id.

127 **young men consistently lag behind their female peers:** Andrea S. Kramer and Alton B. Harris, "Are U.S. Millennial Men Just as Sexist as Their Dads?," *Harvard Business Review*, June 15, 2016, hbr.org/2016/06/are-u-s-millennial-men-just-as-sexist-as -their-dads.

Chapter Six

137 **three as the "magic number" for both men and women:** Sophie Haslett, "So What IS the Magic Number? The Ideal Number of Sexual Partners for Men and Women Revealed (and It's Fewer Than You Might Think)," *Daily Mail* (London), December 23, 2016, www.dailymail.co.uk/femail/article -4060846/The-ideal-number-sexual-partners-men-women -revealed.html.

137 **twelve as the ideal and nineteen as the upper limit:** Stephanie Linning, "How Many Is TOO Many? Why Men and Women AGREE on the Ideal Number of Sexual Partners (and It's More Than You Expect!)," *Daily Mail* (London), May 4, 2017, www.dailymail.co.uk/femail/article-4472804/Men-women -AGREE-ideal-number-sexual-partners.html#ixzz55zb6rVxP.

138 **an analytical look at the series:** Christy Smith, "In 'Sex and the City,' Number of Sex Partners True to New York Life," *New York Daily News*, May 28, 2008, www.nydailynews.com /entertainment/sex-city-number-sex-partners-true-new-york-life -article-1.326644.

141 **A particularly noxious display of this belief:** "Shelly Donahue's Abstinence Education WAIT Training (Clip 1)," YouTube, December 17, 2012, www.youtube.com/watch?v =enCIs-0Iebc.

142　**publications as diverse as *Jezebel, Men's Health, Slate,***
　　　***Psychology Today,* and *LA Weekly*:** Tracy Moore, "A Primer on
　　　What Sex Does (and Doesn't) Do to Your Vagina and Butthole,"
　　　Jezebel, May 11, 2013, jezebel.com/a-primer-on-what-sex-does-and
　　　-doesnt-do-to-your-vagin-500204347; Carrie Borzillo, "How Many
　　　of These Vagina Urban Myths Do You Believe?," *Men's Health*,
　　　January 26, 2015, www.menshealth.com/sex-women/vagina-urban
　　　-myths; Christina Cauterucci, "Does Lots of Sex Change a Vagina's
　　　Size and the Labia's Color? Reddit Answers," *Slate*, January 26,
　　　2016, www.slate.com/blogs/xx_factor/2016/01/26/does_lots_of
　　　_sex_change_a_vagina_s_size_and_the_labia_s_color_reddit
　　　_answers.html; Michael Castleman, "The Rare Truth About 'Tight'
　　　and 'Loose' Women," *Psychology Today*, September 16, 2011, www
　　　.psychologytoday.com/blog/all-about-sex/201109/the-rare-truth
　　　-about-tight-and-loose-women; Melysa Martinez, "Demystifying
　　　the Vagina: Does Too Much Sex Make Her 'Loose'?," *LA Weekly*,
　　　October 3, 2011, www.laweekly.com/news/demystifying-the
　　　-vagina-does-too-much-sex-make-her-loose-2530297.

150　**in January 2012, Nixon notes:** Alex Witchel, "Life After 'Sex',"
　　　New York Times, January 19, 2012, www.nytimes.com/2012/01
　　　/22/magazine/cynthia-nixon-wit.html.

151　**Nixon is further pressed to clarify:** Kevin Sessums, "Cynthia
　　　Nixon on Bisexuality & Her New Role in 'Wit,'" *Daily Beast*,
　　　January 24, 2012, www.thedailybeast.com/cynthia-nixon-on
　　　-bisexuality-and-her-new-role-in-wit.

Chapter Seven

158　**the tactic has popped up in a diverse range of movies:** "The
　　　Baby Trap," TV Tropes, tvtropes.org/pmwiki/pmwiki.php/Main
　　　/TheBabyTrap, accessed February 4, 2018.

159　**The American Congress of Obstetrics and Gynecology**
　　　specifically defines: "Committee Opinion Number 554,"
　　　American Congress of Obstetrics and Gynecology, February
　　　2013, www.acog.org/Clinical-Guidance-and-Publications
　　　/Committee-Opinions/Committee-on-Health-Care-for
　　　-Underserved-Women/Reproductive-and-Sexual-Coercion.

159　**a "male behavior.":** Tracy Clark-Flory, "Hidden Pills and Broken
　　　Condoms: The Reality of Reproductive Coercion," *Vocativ*,

October 12, 2016, www.vocativ.com/367040/hidden-pills-and
-broken-condoms-reproductive-coercion.

159 **an overview of literature about reproductive coercion:**
Jeanna Park, Sherry K. Nordstrom, Kathleen M. Weber, and Tracy
Irwin, "Reproductive Coercion: Uncloaking an Imbalance of
Social Power," *American Journal of Obstetrics and Gynecology* 214,
no. 1 (January 2016): 74–78.

160 **Some argue that concealed ovulation arose:** Jared Diamond,
"Sex and the Female Agenda," *Discover Magazine*, September 1,
1993, discovermagazine.com/1993/sep/sexandthefemalea262.

160 **concealed ovulation is a way for the reproductive
imperative:** Nancy Burley, "The Evolution of Concealed
Ovulation," *American Naturalist* 114, no. 6 (December 1979):
835–858.

161 **detractors deemed the work "gruesome and
pornographic,":** Charles Lane, "The Art of Folly at Yale,"
Washington Post, May 3, 2008, www.washingtonpost.com
/wp-dyn/content/article/2008/05/02/AR2008050202795.html.

161 **deriding Shvarts herself as "insensitive":** Samantha
Broussard-Wilson, "Reaction to Shvarts: Outrage, Shock, Disgust,"
Yale Daily News, April 18, 2008, yaledailynews.com/blog/2008
/04/18/reaction-to-shvarts-outrage-shock-disgust.

161 **Wanda Franz, the president of the National Right to Life:**
Catherine Donaldson-Evans, "Yale Officials Conclude Student's
Shocking Claim of 'Abortion Art' Was 'Creative Fiction,'" *Fox
News*, April 17, 2008, www.foxnews.com/story/2008/04/17/yale
-officials-conclude-student-shocking-claim-abortion-art-was
-creative.html.

162 **deeming the work a "creative fiction,":** Tom Leonard,
"Abortion Art a Hoax, Claims University," *Telegraph* (London),
April 17, 2008, www.telegraph.co.uk/news/worldnews/1895884
/Abortion-art-a-hoax-claims-university.html.

167 **first began appearing in women's media:** De Elizabeth,
"Switzerland Court Determined 'Stealthing' Is Not Rape," *Teen
Vogue*, April 22, 2017, www.teenvogue.com/story/new-study
-documents-sex-trend-stealthing.

167 **publications like *USA Today*, the *New York Post*, and *Forbes*:**
Eric Glasser, "A Disturbing Sex Trend Called 'Stealthing' Is on the
Rise," *USA Today*, April 26, 2017, www.usatoday.com/story

/news/nation-now/2017/04/26/disturbing-sex-trend-called
-stealthing-rise/100921352; Lauren Tousignant, "'Stealthing' Is
the Newest Dangerous Sex Trend," *New York Post*, April 24, 2017,
nypost.com/2017/04/24/stealthing-is-the-newest-dangerous
-sex-trend; Robert Glatter, "'Stealthing': The Disturbing New Sex
Trend You Need to Know About," *Forbes*, April 29, 2017, www
.forbes.com/sites/robertglatter/2017/04/29/stealthing-the
-disturbing-new-sex-trend-you-need-to-know-about
/#3c454df71b07.

167   **The initial source of all this interest?:** Alexandra Brodsky,
"'Rape-Adjacent': Imagining Legal Responses to Nonconsensual
Condom Removal," *Columbia Journal of Gender and Law* 32, no. 2
(2017): 183–210.

170   **Other strategies young men employ to coerce:** Kelly Cue
Davis, Trevor J. Schraufnagel, Kelly F. Kajumulo, Amanda K.
Gilmore, Jeanette Norris, and William H. George, "A Qualitative
Examination of Men's Condom Use Attitudes and Resistance: 'It's
Just a Part of the Game,'" *Archives of Sexual Behavior* 43, no. 3
(April 2014): 631–643.

174   **an episode of *The Wendy Williams Show*:** "Ask Wendy: I Want
Another Baby!," *The Wendy Williams Show*, April 22, 2014, www
.youtube.com/watch?v=5CNHwhHWPoQ.

175   **estimated rates as high as 25 percent:** Park, Nordstrom,
Weber, and Irwin, "Reproductive Coercion."

175   **estimating that 10.4 percent of men:** Park, Nordstrom, Weber,
and Irwin, "Reproductive Coercion."

182   **In North Carolina, a woman's ability to withdraw consent:**
Erik Ortiz, "North Carolina Legal Loophole Prevents Women
from Withdrawing Consent to Sex," *NBC News*, June 23, 2017,
www.nbcnews.com/news/us-news/north-carolina-legal-loophole
-says-women-can-t-withdraw-consent-n776026.

Chapter Eight

184   **straight men are 3.5 times more likely:** Kelly Cooper, "A
Woman's Advantage," OkCupid, March 5, 2015, theblog.okcupid
.com/a-womans-advantage-82d5074dde2d.

184   **[Footnote 1] The fact that competitor Bumble requires:**
Alison Segel, "Why Women Should Message Guys First, According

to Bumble CEO Whitney Wolfe," *Elite Daily*, June 27, 2017, www
.elitedaily.com/dating/women-bumble-dating/2003863.

184 **woman-initiated proposals still rare enough:** Alix Strauss,
"Why Women Proposing Is Still Rare," *New York Times*, February
25, 2016, www.nytimes.com/2016/02/28/fashion/weddings
/women-proposing-leap-year.html.

184 **only 18 percent of women had purchased condoms:** Zach
Schonbrun, "XOXO Campaign: Will It Spell Profit or Trouble for
Condom Maker?," *New York Times*, April 23, 2017, www.nytimes
.com/2017/04/23/business/media/xoxo-campaign-will-it-spell
-profit-or-trouble-for-condom-maker.html.

188 **Chivers recorded women showing a genital response:**
Meredith Chivers, Michael C. Seto, and Ray Blanchard, "Gender
and Sexual Orientation Differences in Sexual Response to Sexual
Activities Versus Gender of Actors in Sexual Films," *Journal of
Personality and Social Psychology* 93, no. 6 (2007): 1108–1121.

189 **the *New York Times Magazine* profiled Chivers's research:**
Daniel Bergner, "What Do Women Want?," *New York Times*,
January 22, 2009, www.nytimes.com/2009/01/25/magazine
/25desire-t.html.

189 **[Footnote 3]compared to a 2008 piece that ran in the *Times*
Styles:** Andy Newman, "What Women Want (Maybe)," *New York
Times*, June 12, 2008, www.nytimes.com/2008/06/12/fashion
/12bisex.html.

191 **Cara Anaya, a PGAD sufferer:** "Up to 180 Orgasms in Two
Hours: Woman Living with Persistent Genital Arousal Disorder,"
Barcroft TV, November 17, 2014, www.youtube.com/watch?time
_continue = 15&v = E-jFl6x1Ny8.

191 **somewhere between 4 and 5 percent of rape survivors:** Roy
Jerome Levin and Willy T. M. van Berlo, "Sexual Arousal and
Orgasm in Subjects Who Experience Forced or Non-Consensual
Sexual Stimulation—A Review," *Journal of Clinical Forensic
Medicine* 8, no. 2 (May 2004): 82–88.

192 **documented cases of vaginas lubricating, labia swelling:**
Meredith L. Chivers, Michael C. Seto, Martin L. Lalumière, Ellen
Laan, and Teresa Grimbos, "Agreement of Self-Reported and
Genital Measures of Sexual Arousal in Men and Women: A Meta-
Analysis," *Archives of Sexual Behavior* 39, no. 1 (February 2010):
5–56.

192   **all without any of that registering as arousal for the brain:**
       August McLaughlin, "Are You Orgasming Without Even Knowing
       It?," *Cosmopolitan*, March 14, 2016, www.cosmopolitan.com/sex
       -love/news/a55128/what-i-learned-from-orgasming-in-an-mri
       -machine.

192   **aren't reflected by tools measuring their blood flow and
       brain activity:** Dr. Nicole Prause, conversation with author, May
       19, 2017.

195   **male critics reacted viciously:** Peter Martin, "The *Girls* Recap
       for Men: Self-Indulgent Dreaming," *Esquire,* February 10, 2013,
       www.esquire.com/entertainment/tv/a19304/girls-season-2
       -episode-5-recap.

195   **"the worst episode of *Girls* ever.":** David Haugland and Daniel
       Engber, "Was That the Worst Episode of *Girls* Ever?," Slate,
       February 10, 2013, www.slate.com/articles/arts/tv_club/features
       /2013/girls_season_2/week_5/girls_on_hbo_one_man_s_trash
       _episode_5_of_season_2_reviewed_by_guys.html.

195   **"the fiercest take on female sexuality of [2014],":** Derrick
       Clifton, "Nicki Minaj's 'Anaconda' Is the Fiercest Take on Female
       Sexuality of the Year," *Mic*, August 4, 2014, mic.com/articles
       /95520/nicki-minaj-s-anaconda-is-the-fiercest-take-on-female
       -sexuality-of-the-year#.BdEP2nkme.

198   **feminist blog Babe.net published an account:** Katie Way, "I
       Went on a Date with Aziz Ansari. It Turned into the Worst Night
       of My Life," Babe.net, January 13, 2018, babe.net/2018/01/13
       /aziz-ansari-28355.

199   **In a 2015 essay for *Matter*:** Charlotte Shane, "Swipe Right on
       Monogamy," *Matter*, December 22, 2015, medium.com/matter
       /swipe-right-on-monogamy-189b55568c0c.

201   **Carole Pateman argues that:** Carole Pateman, "Women and
       Consent," *Political Theory* 8, no. 2 (May 1980):149–168.

201   **expounds on the flawed nature of our model of consent:**
       Emma Sulkowicz, "Truth Inside, Truth Outside," The 8th Floor,
       March 24, 2015, the8thfloor.org/wp-content/uploads/2017/03
       /Sulkowicz.pdf.

205   **co-showrunners Lena Dunham and Jenni Konner:** Ryan
       Parker, "'Girls' Writer Murray Miller Accused of Sexually
       Assaulting Actress Aurora Perrineau," *Hollywood Reporter*,
       November 17, 2017, www.hollywoodreporter.com/news/girls

-writer-murray-miller-accused-sexually-assaulting-actress-aurora
-perrineau-1059660.

206 **[Footnote 7] Dunham had tweeted that women don't lie
     about rape:** Lena Dunham (@lenadunham), Twitter, August 4,
     2017, twitter.com/lenadunham/status/893566035638407168.

206 **[Footnote 7] Dunham apologized shortly after defending
     Miller:** Lena Dunham (@lenadunham), Twitter, November 18,
     2017, twitter.com/lenadunham/status/932050109121970176.

206 **Sandra Newman summarizes the existing research:** Sandra
     Newman, "What Kind of Person Makes False Rape Accusations?,"
     Quartz, May 11, 2017, qz.com/980766/the-truth-about-false-rape
     -accusations.

Conclusion

210 *New York Magazine* **described the work as "radical
     vulnerability":** Jerry Saltz, "The 19 Best Art Shows of 2014,"
     New York Magazine, December 10, 2014, www.vulture.com/2014
     /12/19-best-art-shows-of-2014.html.

210 **the** *National Review* **derided Sulkowicz as a "pitiable poet":**
     Ian Tuttle, "'Mattress Girl' Is a Perfect Icon for the Feminist Left,"
     National Review, May 20, 2015, www.nationalreview.com/article
     /418686/mattress-girl-perfect-icon-feminist-left-ian-tuttle.

211 **posters featuring a photo of Sulkowicz:** Taylor Maycan,
     "Posters on, Around Columbia Campus Dub Emma Sulkowicz a
     'Pretty Little Liar'," *USA Today*, May 20, 2015, college.usatoday
     .com/2015/05/20/posters-at-columbia-univ-call-emma-sulkowicz
     -a-pretty-little-liar.

212 **"a disturbing sex tape,":** Natasha Vargas-Cooper, "Emma
     Sulkowicz's Newest Art Project Is a Disturbing Sex Tape," *Jezebel*,
     June 5, 2015, jezebel.com/emma-sulkowiczs-newest-art-project
     -is-a-disturbing-sex-1709234401.

212 **"unsettling and thought-provoking,":** Emma Cueto, "Emma
     Sulkowicz's 'Ceci N'est Pas Un Viol' Art Piece Is Unsettling and
     Thought-Provoking," *Bustle*, June 5, 2015, www.bustle.com
     /articles/88245-emma-sulkowiczs-ceci-nest-pas-un-viol-art-piece
     -is-unsettling-and-thought-provoking.

213 **"troubling.":** Cait Munro, "Emma Sulkowicz Breaks New
     Ground with Troubling Video Performance," Artnet, June 4, 2015,

news.artnet.com/art-world/emma-sulkowiczs-rape-referencing
-video-305180.

213   **That's the version of the story peddled by:** Cathy Young,
      "Columbia Student: I Didn't Rape Her," *Daily Beast*, February 3,
      2015, www.thedailybeast.com/columbia-student-i-didnt-rape-her.

213   **Columbia University's decision to settle a Title IX lawsuit:**
      T. Rees Shapiro, "Columbia University Settles Title IX Lawsuit
      with Former Student Involving 'Mattress Girl' Case," *Washington
      Post*, July 13, 2017, www.washingtonpost.com/news/grade-point
      /wp/2017/07/13/columbia-university-settles-title-ix-lawsuit-with
      -former-student-involving-mattress-girl-case.

215   **an exposé of powerful Hollywood executive Harvey
      Weinstein:** Jodi Kantor and Megan Twohey, "Harvey Weinstein
      Paid Off Sexual Harassment Accusers for Decades," *New York
      Times*, October 5, 2017, www.nytimes.com/2017/10/05/us/harvey
      -weinstein-harassment-allegations.html.

215   **a piece by Ronan Farrow:** Ronan Farrow, "From Aggressive
      Overtures to Sexual Assault: Harvey Weinstein's Accusers Tell
      Their Stories," *New Yorker*, October 23, 2017, www.newyorker
      .com/news/news-desk/from-aggressive-overtures-to-sexual
      -assault-harvey-weinsteins-accusers-tell-their-stories.

216   **Louis CK, who'd long denied rumors about his abusive
      proclivities:** "Louis C.K. Responds to Accusations: 'These Stories
      Are True,'" *New York Times*, November 10, 2017, www.nytimes
      .com/2017/11/10/arts/television/louis-ck-statement.html.

216   **Dan Harmon engaged in a very public back-and-forth:**
      Sonia Rao, "He Harassed Her. She Called Him Out. He Broadcast
      His Apology. She Accepted.," *Washington Post*, January 11, 2018,
      www.washingtonpost.com/news/arts-and-entertainment/wp
      /2018/01/11/he-harassed-her-she-called-him-out-he-broadcast-his
      -apology-she-accepted.

217   **Lindy West notes that:** Lindy West, "Yes, This Is a Witch Hunt.
      I'm a Witch and I'm Hunting You," *New York Times*, October 17,
      2017, www.nytimes.com/2017/10/17/opinion/columnists
      /weinstein-harassment-witchunt.html.

About the Author

LUX ALPTRAUM IS a writer and producer dedicated to improving our conversation about sex. Her writing has appeared in the *New York Times*, *New York Magazine*, *SELF*, *Vice*, *Cosmopolitan*, and *Hustler* and helped shape Fusion's Peabody-nominated series *Sex.Right.Now. with Cleo Stiller*. She lives in New York City.